True Work

True Work

❖

The Sacred Dimension
of Earning a Living

JUSTINE WILLIS TOMS
AND
MICHAEL TOMS

BELL TOWER ❖ NEW YORK

Grateful acknowledgment is made for the use of the hexagrams 19 and 24
from the Richard Wilhelm translation of the I CHING, © 1950 by
Bollingen Foundation Inc., New York, N.Y. New material copyright
© 1967 by Bollingen Foundation © renewed 1977 by Princeton University
Press. Published by Princeton University Press, Princeton, New Jersey.

Published by Bell Tower, an imprint of Harmony Books,
a division of Crown Publishers, Inc.,
201 East 50th Street, New York, New York 10022.
Member of the Crown Publishing Group.

Random House, Inc. New York, Toronto, London, Sydney, Auckland
http://www.randomhouse.com/

Bell Tower and colophon are trademarks of Crown Publishers, Inc.

Printed in the United States of America

Design by June Bennett-Tantillo

Library of Congress Cataloging-in-Publication Data
Toms, Justine Willis.
True work : the sacred dimension of earning a living / Justine
Willis Toms and Michael Toms. — 1st ed.
p. cm.
1. Work—Religious aspects. I. Toms, Michael. II. Title.
BL65.W67T66 1998
291.1'785—DC21 97-20408
CIP
ISBN 0-517-70587-7

10 9 8 7 6 5 4 3 2 1

First Edition

This book is dedicated to Michael Toms, Jr.
(1961–1994),
who left this life too soon,
his children, Meghan and Jeremy,
who continue to remind us as grandparents
why we are doing what we do,
and to our son, Robert Welch,
who is actively pursuing his own true work.

Acknowledgments

We want to acknowledge all of our past coworkers over the years who have planted seeds, nurtured, and watched them grow in the garden called New Dimensions Radio. Thanks to our present coworkers, who have labored with dedication befitting true work while we have been writing this book: Rose Holland, Debbie Pollock, David Hulse-Stephens, Dan Drasin, Jeff Wessman, Mel Baker, Jacqui Dunne, Susan Newstead, Mary Buckley, and Joanne LaCasse. You have been our teachers and we are grateful. Special recognition is due our longtime colleague and friend Tom Greenaway, without whom our work would be considerably less, and who has persevered at our side through the low places and has helped us climb higher on the mountain than we ever thought possible.

To all of those ordinary individuals doing extraordinary things in the world and who have graced us with their presence in our broadcast studio and shared their stories with us on the radio, we feel privileged to be able to work with you.

To our spiritual teachers, each of whom has had a deep influence and holds a special place in our hearts, we are very thankful: Haridas Chaudhuri, Swami Sivananda Radha, J. Krishnamurti, Sogyal Rinpoche, Thomas Merton, Tai Situ Rinpoche, and Tarthang Tulku.

We have been blessed in our lives to know several persons who have become spiritual friends and mentors, who have been there for us when needed, and whose work continues to inspirit ours in the world: Patricia Sun, Robert Fuller,

Richard Moss, M.D., Fr. Jerome Ebacher, Jean Houston, Ron Rattner, the late Joseph Campbell, the late Buckminster Fuller, Barbara Marx Hubbard, Sedonia Cahill, Cheri Quincy, Joel Alter, Judy and Charles Tart, and Arny and Amy Mindell.

Thanks to the New Dimensions Foundation Board of Directors for graciously granting us the time to work on this book and for allowing us access to the New Dimensions Radio archives.

Homage to Jim Hill, who was present at and midwifed the birth of New Dimensions and whose karmic connection we have experienced with awe at pivotal places along the way. Thanks to our treasured friend Abigail Johnston, who gave us valued feedback on the book.

Our gratitude goes to all those dear friends who have patiently borne challenging aspects of our journey in the midst of the circle: members of the Heart Lodge, the Weasel Lodge, the Duncan Springs Circle, the Great Round, the Spider Lodge, the Hot Potatoes, and the Owl-Eagle Lodge.

Singular appreciation goes to our indefatigable editor, Toinette Lippe, who from the beginning has enthusiastically supported the book and cajoled and pushed us to go deeper. She helped us write a better book, and no editor can do more.

Contents

True Work

What Is

True

Work?

*You must remember that
the aim of all work is simply
to bring out the power of the
mind which is already there,
to wake up the soul.*
— Swami Vivekananda

*Work is the only thing that
gives substance to life.*
— Albert Einstein

*If you follow your bliss,
you put yourself on a kind
of track, which has been
there all the while, waiting
for you, and the life that
you ought to be living is
the one you are living.*
— Joseph Campbell

*To love what you do and feel
that it matters — how could
anything be more fun?*
— Katharine Graham

"The smell of eggs frying still lingers in my memory. He was busy making his lunch for work while at the same time cooking breakfast in the kitchen. Through the window, the darkness of early morning was beginning to lighten. As a sleepy five-year-old, I was still in my pajamas and had left the warm comfort of bed to be with Pop, the affectionate name I used for my grandfather, while he prepared for the oncoming day.

"He was muttering partly to himself and partly to me about his dislike of having to go to work at the Bureau of Engraving and Printing in Washington, D.C., where he was a plate printer making paper money. Then he hit his bald head on an open cupboard door as he rose from crouching in front of the lower cabinet near the sink. I remember he gave a yell and proceeded to let forth a diatribe about his job and why he shouldn't have to go to work."

This was Michael's first conscious recollection of work and the fact that his grandfather, whom he loved dearly, did something other than hold him on his knee and tell stories. At the time Michael was puzzled why his grandfather would do something he seemed so set against, and he questioned him, "Why do you go to work, Pop?" Recovering quickly from his angry outburst, his grandfather gently replied, "Because I have to."

Michael can remember noting at the time that when he grew up and "had to" work, he would choose something that he liked doing and that didn't make him angry. Some would say this incident was a relatively harmless childhood encounter with little significance. Later, when Michael became a teenager, his parents separated and his mother was forced to return to work for the first time since he was born. She was not pleased with this turn of events and over the next few years often remonstrated with Michael, "Wait until you have to go to work. You'll find out how hard it is." He recalls thinking to himself at the time, *You just wait. I'll do fine.* And so Michael's inner alarm was set to alert him when the appropriate time arrived and he had to choose work for himself.

These two early family experiences were important catalysts that helped form Michael's attitude and perspective about work and later led him to believe strongly that it was possible, indeed crucial, to do what you love and love what you do.

Justine's grandfather, Harry Herzfeld, was president of a bank in a small town in Alabama. He inherited his job from his father, who had founded the bank. Papa, as he was affectionately called by his four daughters and thirteen grandchildren, always had time for children in his work. Justine recalls, "We would descend on the bank in a tribe, four to six of us at a time. Papa always welcomed us into his office, no matter what business he was conducting at the moment. After he had proudly introduced us to whoever was there, we helped ourselves to Dubble Bubble gum, which he kept in the bottom right-hand drawer of his enormous desk. Then he would give each of us a nickel to buy a soft drink.

"Papa included us on long rides in the country when he visited farmers to talk about loans. We played in front yards, which rarely supported grass but were always swept clean like a Zen garden. Papa sat on the front porch with other elders, and for hours they told stories about days past. Whenever they came to someone's name, they would inevitably speak that person's lineage. Their conversation would go something like this:

"The farmer would say, 'Before they built the dam, the Tallapoosa used to run by Harold Parrish's place.'

"And Papa would reply, 'Oh, yes, he was one of the Parrish boys who came down from Anniston. I knew his father, Mr. Max Parrish, who worked on halves on Mr. Ocie Warren's farm. Mr. Max's wife was a Carlisle from Clay County. . . .'

"This conversation was the chant I grew up with. Only in recent years have I come to appreciate how these visits formed the warp and woof of that society." The late journalist and chronicler Sir Laurens van der Post reminds us that this kind of chant goes back to the first peoples: "He [the Bushman] knew intuitively that without story one had no clan or family; without a story of one's own, no individual life; without a story of stories, no life-giving continuity with the beginning, and therefore no future. Life for him was living a story."

Justine's grandfather was a good friend to farmers and others who struggled to eke out an existence in the rural South. He used his power and influence as a financier to help others and had bestowed upon him Auburn University's Algernon Sydney Sullivan Award for "the highest spiritual and humanitarian qualities practically applied to daily living."

These early memories of our elders' attitudes toward work helped to form our own mental disposition toward work. Although our backgrounds are quite different, we have come to hold a similar view about work.

It is our experience that work and life are inextricably connected because both are driven by spirit. Work has become our spiritual practice and continually provides the opportunity to deepen and enrich our lives. We believe that work is more than a job to make money or to achieve some goal, although it can encompass both these aims.

Getting up in the morning and feeling good about starting the day, having a sense of the contribution you are making through what you are doing—these give meaning to your work and act as a catalyst to propel your work forward. And knowing that your work is providing a useful service to others goes a long way toward softening difficulties or problems that may be associated with your job.

Our friend Marsha Sinetar, author of *Do What You Love, the Money Will Follow*, says, "When our jobs are more to us than just a means to earn a living, our talents, preferences, and true disposition come to life." We agree wholeheartedly. When work is done with commitment and caring, purpose and passion, the best parts of ourselves are summoned forth and the inner light of being shines through our actions.

How we approach life is governed by our attitude and perspective. If our outlook is negative, focused on what doesn't work, colored by cynicism and generally bleak, then it will be that much more difficult to discover and live our passion.

On the other hand, if we have a sense of gratitude, are generally hopeful, engage life with optimism, and have a healthy appreciation of the possibilities inherent in every situation, then we are better equipped to be open to finding our true path and following it with gusto.

Wayne Dyer has said, "Whatever reality you find yourself in, whatever is 'your separate reality,' it is capable of being altered by you at any time that you want. It is not altered by changing what is outside of you; it's altered by changing how you choose to process your life."

There are many who would say it is all a matter of discovering what you love and doing that. If it were that easy, we would all be living our passion and following our dream. What you are about to read has to do with what we have learned through our own experience (and that of hundreds of others we have come to know) about making a life while making a living. It is about how we have learned that work can be sacred. It is about learning to listen and hear the call, finding your true vocation, and making it a part of your life.

We are not experts, but students of the craft of doing what you love. We have found our passion, and are writing this book with the hope that it will help you find yours as well.

In this first chapter we will be setting the stage and giving an overview of the work climate in the postindustrial age. In the chapters that follow we will share some keys to help light the way toward deepening the connection between work and spiritual expression.

The Old Way of Work

Most of us who were raised and schooled in American society were taught that we should decide on a career or a profession before we graduated from high school. We can recall being asked, even when we were very young, "What do you want to be when you grow up?" The idea that we were supposed to *be something* was drummed into us early on.

Michael can remember the career counselor at his college preparatory school saying, "Since you performed better on the mathematical section of the college board exams, you should consider becoming an engineer." His personal leanings were away from math and much more toward creative writing and the arts. Still, he found himself in the school library looking up various engineering careers, and he eventually decided that aeronautical engineering seemed the most interesting. Looking back, he can see that wanting to know how to fly was symbolic of part of what was driving him — but that metaphorical interest had little to do with building airplanes.

This impulse to expand into newness may feel like discontent. The Reverend Mary Manin Morrissey, the author of *Building Your Field of Dreams*, says, "Our discontent is actually a gift of spirit.... As I have learned to honor the discontent, it has always been the doorway into the next dimension of life." This divine discontent is the internal generator that gives us the power to act on our dreams. We have only to tap into it, make friends with it, and allow it to flow within and from us into our chosen work.

If we begin with *being*, then everything we do will encompass our whole self. When *having* is the impetus, then the doing is influenced by material concerns, which can never enable us to live our passion. One reason so many people are dissatisfied and unhappy with their work is that they begin by seeking to *have* rather than to *be*. When *being* informs our actions, self-assurance and inner strength will permeate what we do. By focusing on *being,* we can feel the connection to all life. Work becomes a living, moment-to-moment process in which meaning is ever-present.

The industrial and technological age has done much to alter the workplace. Not the least of its influence has been the virtual extinction of the artist/craftsperson, who valued the process of his or her work as much as (if not more than) the product. The experience of doing the work was as important as the result of the work itself. Now the artist/worker has become an employee in a job, for the purpose of achieving and surviving. The linear ladder of success, based on reaching a series of goals, is the operable image, and spirit and soul are lost in the course of the doing.

So often the workplace is one-dimensional and does not ask us to live in the fullness of our being. It's up to us to listen and feel as deeply as possible so that our soul can speak to us. In *Care of the Soul,* Thomas Moore writes, "Soul is not a thing, but a quality or a dimension of experiencing life and ourselves. It has to do with depth, value, relatedness, heart and personal substance.... It is impossible to define precisely what the soul is. Definition is an intellectual enterprise anyway; the soul prefers to imagine."

Though there is a movement to recover creativity and spirit within the corporate organizational structure, this is still an embryonic movement. By and large, the vast American corporate workplace is populated by dependent employees who fear downsizing and are unable to express their creativity; as a result, they eagerly embrace the TGIF ("Thank God It's Friday") mentality.

It is easy to understand why there is so much worker dissatisfaction on the job when you survey the overall workplace. Recently a large California bank eliminated all health insurance, retirement plans, seniority, and other benefits for its tellers, as well as reducing their wage scale. The employees were offered two alternatives: They could accept the dictates of the employer or find themselves another job.

Worker dissatisfaction is not only rooted in bad treatment by employers. In many cases it goes much deeper, to the essential nature of the work environment. One of the constant laments we hear in our seminars is that people feel unappreciated and unacknowledged for their contributions in the workplace. Sometimes the most valuable and dedicated employees are simply ignored in the overall rush of business as usual, where more attention is given to the ultimate goals than to those who are integral to reaching them. Is it any wonder that many employees are disgruntled, that they feel they are just marking time or there is no purpose in their work?

The New World of Work

For much of the twentieth century, working in America meant a full-time job, which sometimes included benefits and a retirement plan. It also meant having a profession or at least a clearly defined job description. Job security was the expectation, even the "right," of the American worker. Now, though, as companies struggle to survive and maintain their bottom line, long-term, full employment in all industries is slowly disappearing.

Downsizing, job sharing, telecommuting, new technologies, and more are radically altering the workplace. What we were taught in school about work and career is turning out to be very different from the reality. The rigid "rules" of society are breaking down and becoming fluid out of necessity. At no time in modern history have so many human beings been in a position to shift the fundamental assumptions by which they have been living and working. As the old system disintegrates, people are finding themselves out of work, and all their worst fears are realized. However, when there is nothing left to lose, there comes a freedom of choice—a freedom to choose again.

There is a sense of momentum created by so many people changing their work situations. We can grow beyond the assumptions that have been binding us in dull and oppressive occupations. Doors are wide open. We must take the initiative and choose to step through them into new ways of being. Indeed, each of us must choose this, for we are living in a burning barn. And unlike horses that stay in the "safety" of their stalls and burn to death, we must gallop away from these small, disintegrating confines and move toward freedom.

The corporate promises of security were always an illusion. Several generations ago, companies presented themselves as families, although often they did not encompass the ethics and values of the family. People separated their lives into work, family, and religion. The realms of family and religion were distinctly separate from the business area.

Michael's great-grandparents came to the United States from Ireland in the late nineteenth century to find work. Their children, his grandparents, placed great emphasis on job security. His grandfather worked in the same job for forty-five years, and his grandmother worked for the telephone company for a similar amount of time. Being assured of employment was extremely important to them. They wanted to feel secure in having a job for the rest of their lives so that they didn't have to worry about earning a living.

They sacrificed a great deal to follow their own career path. Michael's grandfather went to work out of loyalty to his family, as well as for the assurance of benefits, a pension, sick leave, and other tangible rewards. His passion was collecting coins and stamps, and he gave much of his leisure time to that pursuit.

Your Contribution Is Important

No one can know the future. A new kind of loyalty is necessary—one that honors a dynamic, firsthand engagement with life in the moment. The knights of the Round Table went out in search of the Holy Grail, and each entered the forest at its darkest point, "where there was no path." The ability to give our unique gifts to the world comes from following our own path. If we don't follow that course, the world is the poorer for it and *we* are deprived as well. There is no bargaining with the soul. We must embrace it wholly or we will find ourselves living a half-life, one that does not include our originality.

The world needs your creativity. Now is the time for you to make your original contribution. No longer is it appropriate to sit back and let others do everything. The national and global crises we face today demand that each of us do what we can. No matter how small your action may appear, it will have an effect, so don't hold back.

Your experience and wisdom is important as a piece of the overall tapestry. Everything is changing. The fields of health, education, communications, politics, science, travel, social service, media, and finance are undergoing dramatic transformation in countless ways. We're living in the midst of an exciting, exhilarating, and challenging time, ripe for seminal change at many levels. The father of modern psychology, William James, once set himself the dictum, "I will act as if what I do makes a difference." Not only did he change his own life, he affected the lives of millions of others, and his legacy continues long after his death. You'll never know the full power and effect of your actions. But it's crucial that you act.

Soul Moments

So often our life becomes filled with distractions and reasons why we can't live our enthusiasms. But we live at a time when *the opportunities have never been greater,* and the available support for the expression of our personal passion, creativity, and excellence has also never been greater. We must put up our sails and catch the winds that are ready to carry us into unexplored territory. The ego is constantly trying to set up tents and hunker down, but the soul calls us to go around the next bend in the path as it seeks liberation from the bonds that hold us back from living our passion.

Each of us can look back over our lives and notice particularly strong moments that catalyzed a shift in direction. Some event, experience, or chain of circumstances led us to a crossroads, and a life-changing decision was made.

Even though these experiences are often painful, they should be cherished because they give us a window in time to reevaluate the road we are on. Reviewing our life and noticing the turning points can provide a wealth of insights about where we are today and where we may be going tomorrow, because they invariably inform our actions in the moment.

We can recall the late Joseph Campbell speaking to this point when he referred to an essay written by Schopenhauer called "An Apparent Intention of the Fate of the Individual." Campbell said, "He points out that when you are at a certain age—the age I am now (seventy-five)—and look back over your life, it seems to be almost as orderly as a composed novel. And just as in Dickens' novels, little accidental meetings and so forth turn out to be main features in the plot, so in your life. And what seem to have been mistakes at the time, turn out to be directive crises." And then he asked, "Who wrote this novel?" He went on to say that life seems as though it is planned and that there is something inside of us that causes these occurrences. It's a mystery. All of us can look back at our lives and see events that appeared to be disasters at the time but shifted us to a new course and led us into important aspects of our journey. It's as though nothing can happen for which we're not ready.

Living the Great Questions

To help us recognize these crossroads we have found it useful to practice remembering such questions as "Why am I here? What is life really about? What is the purpose of my life? Whom or what do I serve? How have I constructed my life to come to this place? What do I want to contribute to the world?" These core questions serve as reminders, helping us to recall that there's more to life and work than making money and having a job. To make such an inquiry on occasion deepens our spiritual roots and restores our connection with soul.

As you are able to give energy to your passion, purpose will emerge. Clarity of purpose comes from honoring what gives your life meaning. Work has become void of meaning because people are asked to follow instructions rather than their creativity. True work is an expression of following your inner voice, heeding the spiritual call, and living your passion.

Engaging Your Work

In the Thai language there is a word, *sanuk*, which means that whatever you do, you should enjoy it. Without joy or happiness, nothing is worth doing. Sulak Sivaraksa, a Buddhist monk and a leading proponent of what is called "engaged Buddhism," explains, "*Sanuk* means that you enjoy your work with mindfulness and awareness, with respect for others and for nature. *Sanuk* also means that you contribute to the welfare of others. So, with all of your enjoyment, you must also have *dana*—giving, charity. That is essential. If people would practice enjoying themselves with respect for others, that would be a harmonious way of living."

Unifying Work

The attitude that work is "over here" and spiritual life is "over there" prevents us from engaging life to the fullest. We imagine that we are marking time at work and that life begins when we arrive home in the evening or on the weekends. The result is that work is not fully integrated into our days, and we wind up living at the margins of our lives.

There are two important precepts to remember in the practice of true work. First, we must express our gifts no matter what. If we can earn a living doing that, great; if not, we must find a way to contribute these talents in whatever small or large way we can. Second, each of us is in the position to make some meaningful contribution to the life around us. While there will be challenges and problems that will inevitably arise when we put forward in the world what is uniquely ours, for our soul's sake it is important that we do this.

Basically, human beings want satisfaction and fulfillment, and we especially want to feel a sense of accomplishment in what we are doing. Being of service and achieving something of value to others while feeling balanced and healthy are the essential reasons for working. Since most of us spend 60 percent of our waking lives doing it, it's important that we examine the nature of our work.

TWO

❖

Discovering Your Passion

Spirit is passionate; without passion no one can be truly spiritual.

—DEEPAK CHOPRA

The voyage of discovery lies not in finding new landscapes but in having new eyes.

—MARCEL PROUST

Only those who will risk going too far can possibly find out how far one can go.

—T. S. ELIOT

Your work is to discover your work, and then with all your heart to give yourself to it.

—GAUTAMA BUDDHA

One evening in early 1973, we attended a conference called "Frontiers of Consciousness" at the University of California, Berkeley. We were deeply touched by the speakers at that event and by the truth they spoke about the growth of human consciousness. Especially significant were the words of psychologist Charles Tart, who said, "We may be in the most dramatic shift in human consciousness in the history of the planet, and nobody is paying attention."

The next day, sitting around the breakfast table with our friend Jim Hill, we bubbled away about the importance of what we had heard the day before. We wondered aloud, "Why don't we read about this in newspapers or magazines? This is the greatest revolution happening on the planet, and no one is reporting on it."

Jim reflected our fervor back to us with the challenge, "Well, why don't you do something?" We can still feel the excitement that flashed through both of us as that question lit up our hearts. We replied on the spot, "Yes, why don't we?" The next couple of hours were spent imagining the basic structure we wanted to create, and deciding what to call it. The name New Dimensions Foundation felt just right. Because the basic purpose was educational, we decided that forming it as a nonprofit organization would be the most appropriate way to go.

Our vision was to change consciousness by bringing diverse thinkers, social innovators, creative artists, scientists, and spiritual teachers together in public dialogues. The next day we went to see a lawyer and started the ball rolling on incorporation of the nonprofit status. That was in March

1973. In September of the same year we began our radio work, and we have been broadcasting ever since. We had discovered our passion.

Following your passion is both a difficult path and an easy one; it's a paradox. It is difficult because it will lead you into unknown territory. It is easy because you will be doing what you love. Michael took the lead in the beginning, since he knew from experience how to birth and grow an organization. On the one hand, it is all very straightforward; on the other hand, it is an amazing process not unlike childbirth. Instead of going to a medical doctor, one hires a lawyer as midwife. In the eyes of the state, a corporation takes on its own identity with its own tax identification number and it receives a birth certificate with its date of incorporation. Its fingerprints and footprints are its mission statement and articles of incorporation.

The Call

Ask yourself the question, "To what do I most yearn to give my full energy and commitment?" Another way of phrasing this can be found in Jonathan Robinson's book *The Little Book of Big Questions:* "If I knew I could not fail, what would I be doing?" The answer will open you to the territory of your soul's longings.

If you don't have a clear answer to the question, never fear; it will emerge when the time is right and you are ready, just as it did for us. Sometimes we require experience, adventures, challenges, and more to prepare us for the work we are to do. Trust the process of life, give yourself to it fully, and your higher purpose will gradually make itself known to you. To paraphrase an old adage, "The calling will come when the worker is ready." Michael had three professions before being led to his true calling, and all of them provided valuable training for the work he now does.

After high school, before going on to college, he got a job as a trainee technical writer with a research and development firm. This started him thinking seriously about writing as a profession. At the same time he had an inclination toward radio and broadcasting, so at night he went to broadcasting school to learn how to become an announcer.

All the while, he was on a spiritual search with a deep and abiding interest in philosophy and religion. There were three significant influences in Michael's early life that affected his ultimate vocation—Thomas Jefferson, Will Durant's *Pleasures of Philosophy,* and Boswell's *The Life of Samuel Johnson.* Jefferson's comprehensive thinking and vision impressed Michael; Durant's book showed him that the pursuit of knowledge and wisdom could be a lifelong endeavor; and Johnson and his extraordinary circle of friends with their freewheeling and adventurous dialogues were a revelation. It took years of gestation for these influences to resolve themselves ultimately into a clear direction and path for Michael.

Essentials for Success

The underlying principles we've found necessary for any work to be effective can be summed up as: *taking the initiative; engaging your work with energy and enthusiasm; hold-*

ing the future loosely; and *persevering — being willing to hang in there, no matter what.*

When Michael first went into the workplace, he applied himself, taking the initiative, doing things that he wasn't necessarily being told to do. He worked with energy and enthusiasm and tried not to think about the future or worry about where this was going to take him, or what it was going to do for him. In the beginning Michael did not consciously think of what he was doing in these terms; the actions emerged spontaneously from within. Later in life it has become obvious that these essentials are universal. They inhabit every person's story and are available to all of us.

The Odyssey

Soon after leaving school, Michael was hired by a major multinational corporation to work in sales and marketing. He had no doubt, at that time, that he would spend the rest of his life successfully climbing the corporate ladder. In those days, no one was talking about the soon-to-be reality that we could look forward to not just one career but many careers in a lifetime.

Because Michael was self-directed, it mattered to him only that he be successful on *his* terms, and that meant doing the best he could with whatever task he was given. So that's what he did. With this he began to learn one of the first great lessons in living a successful life.

When he brought his full energy and enthusiasm to the job, people noticed what he was doing and how he was doing it. It also attracted mentors who guided him. After a brief time he was given a promotion and suddenly found himself in a job that previously had been reserved for those with much more experience.

At this point he was in his early twenties. The job enabled him to travel around the United States, visiting major cities. It was a chance to see the country on the company's money and train people to market products to the federal government and the military services.

Thus began his quest. It took a couple of years of patience and perseverance but, again, because he had done the job well, he was in a position in the company where he could say, "Here's what I want." He was able to ask for it and get it. In 1964 he relocated to the San Francisco Bay area, which he had first glimpsed during his business trips. He spent the next few years experiencing the emergence of the rock music scene, coupled with the flower-child, anti–Vietnam War, free-speech, and peace movements, all of which altered his perspective on what he should and could be doing with his life.

His next promotion necessitated moving to southern California. Shortly after accepting the new position and relocating, he became engaged to be married. By this time he had been with the company for seven years and was a rising star in the corporate firmament, with a company car and an expense account plus a great benefits package. The money was flowing, and he was good at what he did. Life was great.

Just when he thought he was in control of his life and destiny, his life abruptly took a U-turn. Five days before the wedding, his fiancée decided that the time was not right to get married, and he reluctantly agreed. When it dawned on him that this was not a temporary situation but a permanent one, he was shocked and deeply saddened.

His whole carefully constructed world dissolved. He was

devastated. It was a period of hopelessness, with nothing to hang on to. He was twenty-seven and had never experienced such disorientation. It was like living in a sci-fi movie in which the hero goes to sleep one night and awakens the next morning to an alien landscape. He didn't speak the language or know the territory. He didn't have a map, and he was alone.

In retrospect, it is clear that this experience, which appeared to be a disaster at the time, was actually a major turning point in his life. It provided an opportunity for him to pause and reflect on his job and the future. To his utter amazement, in looking at his present work, he realized there wasn't anyone at the top of this Fortune 500 company he wanted to emulate. It became obvious to him that he must leave. Simply put, he didn't want to be there anymore.

He wrote a resignation letter, to the great dismay of those in the corporate home office, who were counting on him to join their ranks soon. They did their utmost to persuade him to change his mind. Their words continue to ring in his ears: "How can you sacrifice your career? You have a bright future. You're not thinking right. You're throwing away a brilliant opportunity."

These were people who perhaps had not heeded their own callings. Many of them were unhappy, with failed marriages and nonexistent family lives. Their lives were essentially their jobs. Michael listened politely, didn't argue or try to tell his superiors they were wrong because of what they believed to be correct, and then left.

He also decided to move back to San Francisco and take some time to collect himself and figure out what was next. He was embarking on a new life and what was to become an exhilarating adventure.

Although he didn't know what was ahead nor what he would do in the way of work, the power of the inner voice was so strong that he was compelled to move forward. He can still recall the excitement coursing through his body at the time. It was like entering a spacious room with multiple doors on all the walls and an abundance of light streaming in through wide windows. It was a place of many possibilities — and he was able to choose.

During the next few months it became obvious to him that whatever he did with the rest of his life, he wanted to serve and make a contribution. The dream was beginning to take shape.

What's important is to listen to the call, no matter how distant it may be, and not to let your rational mind get in the way, because it will come up with lots of reasons why your calling won't work or is impossible to attain. Magic happens if you're open to it. This doesn't mean that you should sit on the sidelines and wait for something to occur — quite the contrary. You're part of a creative process, and being able to follow your calling requires your active participation. Only then can you bring your gifts to the world.

Living on credit cards and his wits, Michael was able to take some time off after leaving the corporation. He spent almost a year taking long walks in the park and reading. One day toward the end of this period he was walking in downtown San Francisco, contemplating the immediate future, and asking himself, "How am I going to pay the rent this month?" With no money, fewer prospects, and zero credit left to draw on, he had reached an impasse. Surrendering to the situation, he simply said a prayer: "I give up. I don't know what to do next. Help me." The next instant an inner voice was telling him, "Enter the next building to find a job." A little confused but trusting the message, he did as he was guided and walked into the nearest building, scanned the directory, found the name of an employment agency on the sixth floor, caught the elevator, entered the office, and proceeded to complete a job application. He was told about a sales job in direct mail advertising. The next day he was interviewed for the job and got it. Although it didn't match his expectations about what would occur after undergoing a major life change and spiritual rebirth, later events demonstrated the perfection of what took place.

Most people are not so fortunate as to have a self-created sabbatical. The majority of us must continue to work in some form of job in order to meet the basic necessities, with the eventual aim of finding work more appropriate to what is important and relevant in one's life. This was the case in Justine's first major work experience.

In the sixties, when Justine was a young mother living in the Deep South, her former husband's income did not provide enough to make ends meet, so she sought a job that would provide the highest pay for the least amount of time expended.

She had attended one year of college before becoming pregnant, and the temptation was great to apply for office or retail sales work. But she discovered that the cotton mill paid better wages, so she applied for work there and was hired. For a year Justine did piecework with hundreds of others, mostly women, many of whom had never graduated from high school.

For her it was just a job, and she went into it focused mainly on money. She would count the sweatshirts in order to figure out when she had topped the minimum requirement and was earning extra wages. When several women reached out in friendship, she began to feel that her life was happening in the mill as well as at home.

An older woman who had worked there for more than twenty years began to share with Justine some tricks to make the work faster and easier. There was another woman who did not have a high-school education but knew a great deal about natural medicine and herbs. She had learned all this from her mother, who had been taught by *her* mother, who in turn had learned it from her own mother. Being a young mother herself, Justine found the woman's practical and time-tested advice about remedies for sick children a tremendous help. These were benefits she had not imagined.

The work was also very physical. Right away she noticed how dependent she was on her right hand, and that her left hand was weak and uncoordinated. Justine came to admire the skill of the women around her and took on the challenge of developing her own dexterity. Years later she learned that developing right-left dexterity improves one's health. Research reveals that ambidextrous humans may enjoy a more balanced brain chemistry, which in turn supports a more balanced body.

Because it was physical work, Justine felt a healthy sense of being tired after an eight-hour shift. At the same time she was refreshed in spirit, because the repetitive action required both relaxation and focused attention, which left her soothed and calm.

With hundreds of machines going at the same time, the shop floor was very noisy, so there wasn't much conversation except on breaks. At the time Justine knew absolutely nothing about meditation, but she loved to sing and would spend hours singing simple songs to herself. This helped keep her in rhythm with her machine. Only later was she to discover that for thousands of years people throughout the world have received positive benefits from chanting, often combining it with repetitive work movements.

There were long stretches of time in the work when she would reflect on the future. During those hours she formulated a plan to finish college, which she carried out later, eventually earning a degree in education so that she could teach grade-school children.

Justine describes this period in her life: "It was a time for me to 'make it on my own,' so to speak. People accepted me as I was — and I reciprocated. These relationships were not based on where I was born or who my parents were but on who each of us was in that moment, person to person."

Before the year was over, there was a crowning moment in which she was able to make a positive difference for both herself and others. The policy in that part of the mill was to pay the same wage for regular work as for the more tedious work. All felt the inequity of this, and finally one day Justine stopped her machine, stood up, and went to the supervisor to make a pitch for changing it.

This was a powerful moment for Justine. "I remembered a momentary stillness when I arose, and could feel all the women silently rooting for me as they went back to their work." The outcome was ultimately positive, which served as an initiation for her in experiencing her ability to effect change in the world. The wage scale was increased at just about the time she left the mill for college.

Justine recalls, "I thought I had taken the job simply in

order to earn money, and I went into it with many very negative preconceptions about mill work and assembly lines. Much to my surprise, I learned many skills there, met some interesting people, and made a contribution. All in all, it was a very rich time in my life."

What each of our early work stories reveals is that we were blessed with the confidence that we could choose our future and that whether we were in a cotton mill in Alabama or a Fortune 500 company in San Francisco, we had the grace to make peace with each situation. Neither of us was in our ideal work; nevertheless, we both applied ourselves with energy and enthusiasm to the task at hand.

If you are not in a state of acceptance of where you are, then you are using up your energy battling your current situation. Being in opposition to your work situation will consume valuable life energy, which can be put to much better use following your passion.

Bringing Passion to Your Work

A key to knowing if you are doing what you really want to do is to check out how much passion you bring to the activity. If you are lukewarm about what you're doing, then you can be certain you're not connected to your true calling. It's not that you have to be emotional; it's the inner force you express in your actions that calls forth your fire.

Observe what activity energizes you. Does it serve people and the planet? Do you enjoy doing it? The answers to these questions will help to determine what it is you love to do.

The "joy quotient" is an important factor. Any activity in which your small self or ego-consciousness dissolves, where you find that you become one with the process and time disappears, may point in the right direction. Life provides clues, and the universe wants us to find our niche, but we need to be awake. Because we live in an era teeming with distractions of the most sophisticated kind, it's very easy to become unconscious, lulled and mesmerized into a walking sleep in which we lose our sensitivity to the present moment, where our true power resides.

In this high-speed, technological, and materialist society, ethical and values-based action has become rare. The quest for more security and safety quashes the capacity for caring and compassion. This is all the more reason to act with integrity and not out of our fears about the future. Our work must support and nurture life, and it must come from who we are. It cannot come from those we are imitating or would like to be.

We need not fear this authentic self; we all are drawn to what is good and right for ourselves and for others. Aberrations from this basic natural goodness are like dark clouds at night, which seem to devour the full moon. But just as the moon's light is not, in truth, touched by the clouds, so too our true self is whole and shining and merely needs to be uncovered.

Serving people and the planet are the twin hallmarks of true work. Those who came before us made it possible for us to be here, just as what we're doing now will affect our children's children's children. Native Americans speak of making choices that will be beneficial to the seventh generation to follow.

Being Appropriate

When we probe the inner depths and seek for what is appropriate, a question to ask is, "What needs to be done?"

The late R. Buckminster Fuller ("Bucky," as he was affectionately known) gained renown as an inventor and designer (the Dymaxion House, the Dymaxion Car, the Dymaxion Map), creator of the geodesic dome, coiner of the term "Spaceship Earth," organizer of the World Game, discoverer of Synergetics, and a relentless individualist whose vision and genius continue to reverberate throughout the world. He used to say, "Look for the gaps. Notice what isn't being done, and do that." There is plenty to do. Pay attention, look around, and respond to what calls you. This will ensure the vitality and aliveness of whatever you choose to do, because it is a response to the real life of the world.

The Tibetans have a saying: "If you want to know the future, look at what you're doing in the present." Are we simply marking time, or are we doing what is necessary and appropriate for ourselves and others? The future depends on the actions you take now. Making a contribution to others emerges from the realization that fulfilling your soul's purpose begins with truly loving yourself. "Love thy neighbor as thyself." Often we forget the "thyself" part, and this is frequently the cause of becoming burned out and not being able to sustain the energy necessary for action.

Over time it becomes necessary to remind yourself of the original vision that inspired the work in the first place. Allow yesterday, with all its challenges and paths not taken, to fade; each morning awake and begin anew. Cut loose the baggage of yesterday and arise from a night of rest unencumbered. Daily resurrection and rebirth provide the energy for the present as we create our life afresh and in the moment through our work. Be reborn every day.

Everyone Is an Artist

As a painting calls upon an artist's ability to imagine, so work can call upon your innate artistry. Artist Adriana Diaz says, "Creativity is the real magic of the universe, because we have the power to envision something in our head, in the darkness, pick up any tool that we want, and create that. That is magic. We are conjurers, and we need to see ourselves in that light."

Michael recalls having a three-hour layover in a midwestern airport a few years ago: "Wandering the corridors trying to decide how I would spend the time, I heard a voice singing. I followed the sound to a small room with open doors on either side, which turned out to be a shoeshine parlor. The man shining shoes was happily singing, laughing, and generally uplifting the spirits of all who came within his orbit. Most of us were on the way to somewhere else, rushing around being anywhere but in the moment. This man's whole being was focused in the present as he shined shoes. It was extraordinary, and at the same time it was most ordinary. I had my shoes shined and remained there for about an hour, basking in the positive energy this man exuded through his dedication and singular artistry."

Beauty Nurtures Passion

A sense of beautiful surroundings is an integral aspect of living our passion in the world. The man shining shoes possessed an appreciation of the beauty inherent in his work. His tiny booth was inviting. There was nothing shabby or depressing about his space. It is often forgotten how much easier it is to work in a beautiful environment. The body is more relaxed when surrounded by beauty.

Our assistant, Rose Holland, is able to maintain an island of beauty and spaciousness in her work space. At the end of each day she allows enough time to put everything on her desk away. She often brings in flowers from the garden. Even when the workload is mountainous and details scream for attention, she takes time to stack her papers neatly, taming the unruly mess into an orderly pile.

There have been times when Justine's office has become so crammed with papers and boxes that she finds herself avoiding working in it. Several years ago, recognizing that Justine was overwhelmed by the enormity of the mess, a friend, Sedonia Cahill, offered to come over and help. Sedonia has a wonderful sense of both beauty and utility. The two of them realized that not only did the piles make it difficult for Justine to carry out her work, the entire office arrangement was congested. Soon they were turning the desk around, moving file cabinets, and changing the position of the computer. By placing the desk to face the door, Justine was able to take full command of her office. No longer did people walk in and surprise her as she was engrossed at her desk with her back to the door. She noticed right away that the tension level was reduced and she enjoyed being in her office. They fixed a beautiful space behind her for some art objects and flowers, and this became sacrosanct and free from paper-pile invasion.

Noted author and poet Alice Walker talks about growing up in rural Georgia, where her father was a sharecropper.

"I had a great mother who, around those shacks, planted the most incredible gardens ever, so that in poverty I was surrounded by beauty from birth. Beauty has sustained me through many, many crises."

Welcome the Unexpected

In Western society, we have been conditioned by the illusion that we can control nature. The evidence is clearly to the contrary, as earthquakes, volcanic eruptions, floods, and fires attest. We also carry that false premise into life, operating as if we could control what happens. If you examine your life, you will realize that events and experiences occur that you did not expect to happen. You don't know what may happen in the next moment to change your life. You need to learn to welcome the unexpected. When something happens that surprises, upsets, shocks, astonishes, or amazes you, simply breathe deeply and let go of wanting to control it. Very likely it's impossible to control anyway. Surrender to the experience and realize that whatever is happening, whether you perceive it as a blessing or a curse, it is taking place for some reason and you can learn from the experience. Surprises in life break up the patterns we construct and open us to newness and an awe of life's mystery.

Our friend and coworker, Mary Buckley, felt her life had reached a plateau and she sensed that things needed to change. She wanted to learn how to give herself more deeply in her love relationships and she wanted to change her work situation. She found that the reality of changing her life in these two major areas was both daunting and overwhelming.

Then she was in a serious automobile accident, narrowly escaping death. Having such a close call with death caused her life to change dramatically. She took time off from all her work endeavors and focused on nurturing a new relationship as her body mended. Unexpectedly the accident propelled her into a place where she could start afresh, and she took advantage of it in very healthy ways.

Living with a sense of wonder about the mystery of life creates an atmosphere of possibility. Life is constantly taking us to the brink of chaos. A whole new world of work awaits you if you're willing to open yourself to your deepest longings and purpose. It requires letting go of what you think things are supposed to look like. Learn to expect the unexpected and move forward with radical trust in the process. Our experience tells us that the universe supports risk-taking. Each time we have come to the edge of an abyss, gazed into the unknown depths, and then leaped, we have found an unexpected source of support. As Dorothy Fadiman is fond of saying, "The universe has a matching grant program, but we have to make the jump, and there are no guarantees."

We had an experience, involving our place of work, in which the future opened in the most surprising and unexpected ways. In the early 1980s we were living and working in a five-story building in the middle of San Francisco. We lived with our sons in an apartment on the top floor while the other four floors of the building were devoted to our broadcasting work. On one level were the administrative offices; on another were our tape duplication and mail order operations; the fourth was devoted to a recording studio and an archive. The basement provided a dry place for anything we—and many of our friends and coworkers—wanted to store.

We moved into this building when it was brand-new and occupied it so thoroughly that even though we were renters, we assumed we would always live and work there. Our bubble burst several years later when the owner called one day and said he and his family were planning to move in and take over the top floor.

After having occupied the entire building for over seven years, we could not adjust to the idea of leasing only a portion of the building and having the owner and his family living above us. He was gracious enough to give us a year to find another place. When that year was up and we had not found anything, he extended the lease for another whole year. We kept seeking a space that closely resembled what we had.

It was Michael who spearheaded the search for a new location, finally finding a piece of property in Berkeley that appeared to have all the attributes of the San Francisco building. This time we wanted to purchase it so that we would not be asked to move again. We were convinced we had found the perfect property. It was a four-bedroom house with two levels. Attached to this was a separate two-bedroom apartment, and at the rear of the property there was a two-bedroom cottage. We made an offer, but just when it seemed we had negotiated an agreement with the owners, they asked for something else. Over and over this would happen. We kept agreeing to larger and larger demands by the seller because we were so convinced this was the right place for us. The property offered us such a fine re-creation of our previous place and it had taken us so long to find it. It matched the picture we had of the future. But the future proved surprising beyond our wildest dreams.

One weekend we were visiting friends with whom we had bought an old mineral springs resort located on eighty-eight acres about a hundred miles north of San Francisco. Our friends were living there and we hoped someday to live there also, but we figured it would be many years before we could consider such a move. Justine was lounging in the hammock on Sunday morning and Michael was sitting nearby discussing our dilemma about the Berkeley property when our older son asked us, "What would you *really* want to do if you had all your wishes?" Without hesitation Justine said, "I'd live right here. I'd move up here right now—I wouldn't wait ten years for some time that may never come." Justine remembers the feeling she had when she spoke those words: "I felt my heart leap up in joy. My entire being felt at one with the thought of moving up." Michael was equally positive about the idea.

What was so striking about this was how everything, absolutely everything, fell into place from that moment on. We immediately phoned our colleague Tom Greenaway and told him about our revelation. His response sealed our destiny. He said, "There is a 'For Rent' sign in my apartment building. How about relocating the New Dimensions mail order and tape duplication offices there?" He would coordinate the daily flow from there; we could do the editorial work in the country and be in touch by computer and phone, traveling to the city only when we needed to produce programs in the studio.

And that is exactly what we did. The other key person

was Phil Catalfo, New Dimensions' engineer, station liaison person, and editor of the *New Dimensions Journal*. He was able to work out of his house in Berkeley by making an office space out of a small garage/storage unit on his property, and he was glad not to have to commute. Phil has three children, so coordinating their activities with his wife, Michelle, who also has a job, became much easier. No one had a daily commute, and we all could live exactly where we wanted to live and learn new ways of working together.

A simple question from our son had opened us to splendid new possibilities. With these came the challenge of learning new skills and finding fresh solutions. It broke up old patterns and static ways to which we had been tied.

It is important to realize that the future may not always unfold as you expect.

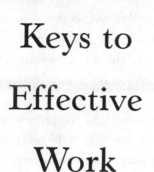

THREE

Keys to Effective Work

Blessed is he who has found his work. Let him ask no other blessedness.
—THOMAS CARLYLE

Most of us have jobs that are too small for our spirits.
—STUDS TERKEL

It does not matter how slowly you go so long as you do not stop.
—CONFUCIUS

Know that it is good to work. Work with love and think of liking it when you do it. It is easy and interesting. It is a privilege. There is nothing hard about it but your anxious vanity and fear of failure.
—BRENDA UELAND

If we could have seen in the beginning all that would eventually be required of us, we might never have begun our New Dimensions work! The beginning of our project was simple, but beginnings do not need to be complex. A newborn baby requires simple things: food, warmth, sleep, love. The baby is not asking for the keys to the car! In a similar way, the initial stage of any worthy project is the time to apply the Law of Baby Steps, which states that it is okay to go slowly.

You may remember playing the children's game "Mother, May I?" One child takes the role of the mother. The other children line up some distance from the mother and, one by one, ask the mother, "May I take a step?" The mother can respond in many ways. She may say no, or she may say, "You may take a giant step," or "You may take a scissor step backward."

The trick is to remember to say "Mother, may I?" after she has given the instructions. If you forget, and you've advanced toward the mother, you must go all the way back to the starting line.

In this game there are many kinds of steps. There are banana steps, giant steps, scissor steps, jump steps, hop-on-one-foot steps, and the smallest of all, the baby step. Justine always wanted to be given a banana step, because it was the biggest one. A banana step is accomplished by lying down with your belly on the ground and stretching out your hands and fingertips. The spot the fingertips reach is where you put your feet next.

Justine's sister, being the oldest, often played the mother. She also had a sense of the trickster. Justine remembers one time when throughout the entire game she was allowed to take only baby steps. Intensely wanting to get ahead of her two brothers, she was disappointed when the mother would say, "Yes, you may take one baby step." However, Justine was diligent in remembering to say, "Mother, may I?" Her brothers would get big steps, but they would get so excited that they would forget the magic words; they had to go back to the starting line over and over. Eventually, much to her delight and surprise, she won that game with her baby steps.

There are many things that make us feel unsafe, such as making mistakes, fear of pain, choosing the wrong thing, losing control, being criticized, and having to make a commitment. These all bring up our defenses. The way to work through this antipathy is by taking one step at a time, starting with the smallest detail. This allows us to focus on smaller elements and not be overcome by the larger picture.

If you are feeling overwhelmed by the enormity of your task, start with what is close to you. For the moment, put the big picture out of your mind and work with what is right in front of you. As you accomplish each step the momentum will build, and gradually the resistance will subside.

Baby steps have an interesting feature—they are connected steps. You place one foot directly in front of the other, heel to toe. There are no great leaps or jumps. Instead, there is a steady, sure, connected movement forward. It is reminiscent of the Tibetan saying "When you go slowly, slowly, you reach fast."

Anything Is Possible

When you open your mind to the idea that everything is possible, it sends a message to the unconscious that there is a limitless horizon. Your attitude and perspective go a long way toward determining the results you get in life and work.

Many athletes use focusing techniques to move themselves past their limits. As a horsewoman who has ridden hunters and jumpers, Justine understands this very well. "As I'm taking a fence, an instructor has often shouted, 'Don't look down; keep your focus up and over the fence, where you want to be. If you look down at the ground, that's where you'll end up.'" So in jumping, keep your focus on where you want to be, not where you don't want to be.

If we see life as the proverbial half-empty water glass, placing emphasis on the negative and everything that's wrong, then life will be filled with negative experiences. On the other hand, if we can see the glass as half full, then life, like a mirror, reflects more positive experiences. It's not that you deny the negative, because it does exist—rather, it's where you place the emphasis.

For some people, life is one big complaint; for others, it is a never-ending banquet of opportunities. You can be one of the latter. When you encounter an obstacle, see it in perspective and work through it, recognizing the learning experience and opportunity it represents. Be tenacious in fulfilling your purpose, and hold the problems and challenges you face with a certain degree of detachment.

So often we define our limits by past experience, and this inhibits breaking through to new levels. Michael remembers when Roger Bannister broke the four-minute-mile "barrier," a barrier that had existed as long as the speed of runners had been officially timed. Yet, within a few months, several others had broken the so-called barrier. In other words, what had previously been impossible became possible.

Miracles happen every day and we simply don't notice them. This is not an arbitrary process. Those who achieve breakthroughs are those who are willing to persevere, make mistakes, and continue to do their work in the face of all manner of obstacles, hindrances, and challenges. Through being consistent and learning from mistakes, it's possible to shatter preconceived limitations and move to higher levels of achievement. This takes practice, and we can practice with little things every day.

As the year is divided into seasons, so our work is marked by different cycles of manifestation. There is winter as well as spring, and we must recognize there will be times when nothing seems to be growing. This is an important time to keep the faith. Our good friend Jack Schwarz, a healer and author of *I Know from My Heart*, says that life is like a roller-coaster ride, and we'd do well to remember not to put on the brakes in the middle of the valley. Stay in touch with your inner voice, and do something—anything—to keep the message of your intention beaming out to both the visible and invisible worlds.

During the slow seasons, refine what you are doing; don't stop in your tracks. By continuing to do something, you will give signals to your own deep self that you are serious about this endeavor, no matter what.

We know of others who, when their expectations were not being fulfilled as fast as they had projected, pulled back and stopped persevering. They used many rationalizations to *not* do something. Some we've heard are: "I need a partner";

"I need to go back to school and get my Ph.D. first"; "I don't have enough money"; "My other obligations are holding me back." Most of these people are still waiting for that perfect time to start—or have abandoned their dreams altogether.

We once worked with someone who had developed an elegant psychological system that helped people live happier lives. He had a marvelous self-help technique to offer. The initial gathering to present his technique in his beautiful home was a huge success, and nearly a hundred people attended. After that the gatherings were smaller and consisted of people who were not just curious, but wanted to change their lives.

However, he became disappointed at the lower turnout, stopped in his tracks, and shut down everything for months at a time. Then, when he began again, it was as if he were starting from scratch. This pattern of self-sabotage kept repeating itself. His energy was soon drained by this, and those who were trying to help him became discouraged as well.

He was unwilling to do what was necessary to manifest his dream. So only a few people were exposed to his teachings, and his large dream died, except where it continues to abide in some smaller form within those of us who were fortunate enough to experience his wisdom.

Synchronicity

Caroline Myss, author of *Anatomy of the Spirit*, tells us that what we choose is not so important as the fact that we have put our full energy and integrity into that choice. "I think what the gods are really looking at is the energy with which we make the decision we do. So whether I choose the right or the left door is, quite frankly, in the Buddhist language, illusion. What matters is what motivated me to choose."

In her book *The Tao of Psychology*, Jean Shinoda Bolen, M.D., writes: "Synchronistic events can assure us when we are on the right life-path, and advise us when we are not; at the most profound level, they reassure us that we are not mere observers, but always participators in an interconnected cosmic web."

Our friend and coworker David Hulse-Stephens gives an example: "You bump into someone in a store you really needed to talk to but weren't able to reach by phone. You were 'coincidentally' brought to the store at the same time as the other person, in a way that is beyond the ability of the rational mind to explain. You could shrug it off as simply a funny coincidence, or you can recognize it for what it is — the mysterious interplay of your powerful unconscious with the physical world."

When Michael found himself in the business of direct mail advertising immediately after going through a spiritual transformation, he questioned whether this was where he should be. The first confirmation came within a few days of his accepting the job, through a phone call from a close friend five hundred miles away who didn't know what he had done. His friend excitedly told him that he wanted Michael to meet a person who was in the direct mail advertising business. Michael saw this as a sign that he should go forward. Later he received other signals that strongly suggested he was on the right track, so he could cease worrying.

Goals and Plans

We all live in an outer-directed society, and we've all been trained to think in terms of objectives, so that our rewards are extrinsic rather than intrinsic to what we are doing. But in truth, life is unfolding in each and every moment. Because our tendency is to set a goal and move toward it, we become more focused on the future than the present.

Having a goal can be a useful tool—but remember that it is just a tool. Since none of us knows what the future holds for us, it is far more effective to live in the present when we work and not to be overly concerned with the future. If you are fully present in the moment, then you will be more effective, and the future will take care of itself. It always does.

We have learned over the years that it can be useful to have a plan, so long as we remember that no plan ever works out quite the way it was envisioned. We can never know all the possible twists and turns that may occur in the future. The value of a plan is that it provides a focus. In order to make your dream happen, it's important to conceptualize it into smaller goal-oriented units and then create a plan for those units. As the specific goals come together, the whole plan takes shape. It's like building a house. First you imagine it and then create a design. Then you build the foundation and frame the walls; gradually the house takes form. The plan gives direction to fulfilling your purpose, minimizes mistakes, and always provides feedback as to the current status of your dream.

Clearly, in the everyday world, you have to plan; but don't become too attached to any one plan. Being wedded to a plan will divorce you from the present. Allow yourself to be open to whatever wants to happen. Unexpected gifts can occur when you're available and not attached to a specific result.

So often it's easy to be distracted or to get caught up in too much planning before you actually move forward—but it's important to follow the path and do something. Allow the path itself to lead you forward. Your task is to do what is necessary in each moment; to trust the process, express your initiative, and throw all of your energy into the work.

If you do this, the rest will take care of itself. Life unfolds naturally and organically if you allow it to do so. This principle, applied to work, will consistently open up new vistas of opportunity.

When we began New Dimensions, the first public occasions we organized were six weekly lectures, comprising a series designed to present many different perspectives on the same topic and yet showing the connections among all the diverse approaches.

It was our intention from the very beginning to record all our work, and we had made arrangements for someone to tape the lecture each week. On the fourth week, the taping person did not appear. He didn't even call to cancel, but left us waiting in the lecture room wondering if he would show up or not. Shortly before the lecture a young man with three companions walked up to us and said, "I just bought a new professional tape recorder, and I'd like to test it out. Do you mind if I tape this lecture?" We were pleasantly surprised, and the synchronicity was not lost on us.

That turned out to be the first of countless special connections that have sustained and supported our work. The young man turned out to be Stephen Hill, who later established the national radio series *Music from the Hearts of Space* and the record company Hearts of Space. His companions were Will Noffke, who had been hosting the radio program *Meeting of the Ways* on a local National Public Radio affiliate station; Eric Anderson, who was also hosting a program on the same station; and Larry Geis. All four people became integral to our work.

After the lecture they joined us for a bite to eat and Eric proposed that we take over his program on the radio. He was ready to move into other interests and liked what New Dimensions represented. He thought it would make a good radio series. The idea of radio had not occurred to us, but it seemed very natural to say, "Yes, we'd love to." Thus we began broadcasting a half-hour program once every other week. Soon that expanded into one hour a week. Then Michael and Will teamed up and served as cohosts of a live, weekly four-hour radio series for five years, with Stephen Hill providing a wealth of expertise in both directing the program technically and sharing his vast knowledge of music. Larry Geis, who is a CPA, continues to lend his financial skills by serving on our board of directors. No one can explain the mystery and magic of such a phenomenal chain of circumstances, but what is clear is that when you act authentically, other forces are unleashed.

When you're holding the future loosely, you bring a certain lightness to your work, which translates into greater flexibility. More choices become available, and you have the freedom to choose what may be a more enlivening direction. Not fixating on the future actually gives you more stability.

In fact, what may appear insecure may actually be more secure. Joseph Campbell once said, "The secure way is really the insecure way, and the way in which the richness of the quest *accumulates* is the right way."

We're reminded of the time when the two of us first got together. Although each of us had a son from a previous relationship, we thought we also would be having children together. The creative impulse was very strong, as it is with so many who come together as a couple. But the time never quite felt right.

Years later, we realized that just about nine months after we got together is when we started New Dimensions. For a quarter of a century we've been creatively working together through *this* vehicle. Clearly this is the "baby" our souls had planned on. If we had held on tightly to our mental picture of the future, we would have had children together, which would have made our life focus very different.

The dream from which our work arises is crucial. We begin from a place of humility, recognizing that what is important is the work itself, not the results of the work. We must constantly guard against becoming attached to the outcome of our work. Beyond the outcome of work are more outcomes, more work, more goals. Therefore the attitude we bring to work is crucial. Knowing that nothing needs to be done is the place from where we begin to move. We release attachment to accomplishing an objective or making something happen in the future; we are present in the moment, working with a pure, energized, and directed focus on the tasks at hand.

This is the secret of what has become known as the science of peak performance, which has enabled many successful individuals to be able to respond quickly to the events around them. Peak performance researcher Charles Garfield writes, "When completely focused on the present, logical and analytical processes are suspended, and as this occurs, the peak performer has the sense that all actions are occurring automatically and effortlessly."

Radical Trust

"Come to the edge," he said.
They said: "We are afraid."
"Come to the edge," he said.
They came.
He pushed them...and they flew.

GUILLAUME APOLLINAIRE

Taking risks is a creative act. There's something special about letting go of the known that is energizing and exciting. It's scary and exhilarating at the same time. There are no guarantees of success, but our experience has demonstrated time and again that somehow everything works out for the best when you surrender and trust the process. What unfolds is usually surprising and very often fulfilling beyond any expectations you may hold. Follow your passion and be in accord with your gifts — joy is a clue. The challenge of entering unknown territory awakes and enlivens the imaginative flow and enables you to engage whatever you encounter along the way with renewed energy and commitment. It won't always be easy, but the rewards will be singularly surprising.

Looking out with positive eyes also requires confidence and faith. You've heard of the power of faith, which is usually related to some religious dictum. We feel that something more than mere faith is required to manifest your passion in the world and empower your work. What's needed is radical trust—the deep knowledge that the universe is ultimately a safe place formed by a loving, creative intelligence. Radical trust allows you to go beyond worry and trivial self-concerns. It's an acceptance of your special place in the overall scheme of things, and the knowledge that each of us is related to the other and capable of making an original contribution to the whole.

Swami Vivekananda said that when you worry, you stop believing in God. "What right have you to bring worry into the world?" he would exclaim. If our worldview is dominated by fears of what will happen, then worry becomes a habit and keeps us from expressing our vision in the world.

With radical trust, you can act clearly in the midst of whatever challenges you may encounter. You accept the reality that there are unseen forces at work, and even though you may not know the eventual impact of your actions, you believe in the process and the ultimate outcome. You're connected to the whole, and the power of the invisible world is available to you. There's solace in this, and it allows you to act from your highest vision.

Using Books as Oracles

One of the many ways to tap into your inner wisdom is through oracles, those prophetic counselors of various forms. We interpret the word *oracle* very loosely. Books, poetry, ani-

mals, trees, or flowers can be oracles—anything that helps us
to reveal the hidden knowledge of divine purpose. For example, have a question in mind, and then take a book of Rumi's
poetry, open it at random to a page, and read the poem as an
oracle in response to your query. An oracle provides a direct
line to our own deep intelligence. It is good to use readings
that give hints but are not explicit, thus leaving room for our
intuition to play a part in the interpretation.

The ancient Chinese oracle, the *I Ching*, or *Book of
Changes*, is an excellent tool for making inquiries; it tells you
what energies are present in a current situation. It has been a
friend of ours for more than twenty years. We don't consult
it often—maybe three or four times a year—but some years,
when change and movement are pressing in on old habits and
ways, the *I Ching* is a much more frequent guest at our table.
Recently a friend who had moved to San Francisco from the
East was facing many questions about work, creativity, living
space, schools—"the full catastrophe," as Zorba would say.
She was also considering taking a job with New Dimensions.
We met with her in the city and discussed some ideas for her,
but it seemed especially important for her to seek advice
from inside herself. As we were leaving to drive the 120 miles
home to Ukiah, Michael suggested that she consult the *I
Ching*. The next morning our friend was on our minds and
we wondered how best to support and integrate her in this
new cycle of our work. Our emotions were running one way,
our logic another, and our hearts a third. So we also decided
to invite the *I Ching* to make a commentary on the situation.

We received a very strong and clear response with
Hexagram 54, *Kuei Mei*, or "The Marrying Maiden":

Thunder over the lake:
The image of THE MARRYING MAIDEN.
Thus the superior (woman) understands the transitory
In the light of the eternity of the end.

The commentary on this particular hexagram described the situation of a new person entering an already existing family unit. Our friend was indeed considering entering a new work situation that involved new relationships.

There was a changing line, so a second hexagram, Hexagram 19, *Lin,* or "Approach," was part of the overall reading:

The Earth above the Lake:
The image of APPROACH.
Thus the superior (woman) is inexhaustible
In (her) will to teach, and without limits
In (her) tolerance and protection of the people.

The reading was encouraging. In the beginning of the relationship there seemed to be an apprenticeship that would ultimately blossom into "creative activity." The Chinese correlate the second hexagram to the end of winter and the very beginning of spring. This changing line had particular significance: "It may appear that the world is passing you by as you wait, but your reward for maintaining your principles is on its way."

Later that day our friend called, and we asked if she had consulted the *I Ching.* She said she felt she had had a very good response, which helped her to see the situation more clearly. Michael then asked what hexagram she had drawn. She said number 54, changing into number 19—the same combination as ours.

We were stunned for a moment. There is a part of us that denies such a thing occurring accidentally, that says, "No big deal—after all, it was a question dealing with the same issue." But we were interested in knowing the odds of such a coincidence. Here we had people 120 miles apart, throwing the *I Ching* within twelve hours of each other, asking a question about the same issue, and getting exactly the same hexagram with the same changing line. So we did a bit of research. There are sixty-four hexagrams, each composed of two trigrams, which consist of three lines apiece. Each line is formed by throwing three coins, and there are four possibilities per throw, and six throws per inquiry. Two statistician friends conferred and confirmed that the odds of any one hexagram appearing twice in two "random" throws are 1 in 4,095! They also said that the odds of that particular hexagram appearing, which spoke so directly to our situation, are 1 in 16,777,216. Our rational process stopped in its tracks. We gave up trying to explain it and moved into the spacious realm of not knowing but feeling the wonder of it all.

Be Flexible

When you combine the spiritual and the intellectual in your work, you develop a natural flexibility that enables you to move quickly and respond to unexpected situations. There will be times when you become mired in the practical unfolding of your work. When this happens, the view becomes one-dimensional and you lose the malleability of movement that allows you to adjust appropriately to challenging circumstances. Without this resilience, spontaneity disappears because the tendency is to stay put and not move. Some of the antidotes to lethargy are prayer, play, walking, exercise of any kind, enjoying the company of children, and being with friends and those who love you. Recognize that it's a temporary phase and will pass.

Another method to help you get unstuck is to review how much you have already accomplished. Bask in the light of all the extraordinary moments that brought you to this point, and know there will be many more.

Being flexible enough to be in the moment with your work and trusting the process allows magic to happen. Magic to us means the unexpected gift that arrives at the perfect time; it could be the solution to a problem or the right person appearing at the right time. Joseph Campbell told us, "I'm not superstitious, but I do believe in spiritual magic. I feel that if one follows what I call one's 'bliss'—the thing that really gets you deep in the gut and that you feel is your life—doors will open up. They do! They have in my life, and they have in many lives that I know of."

Letting Go

Just as it's important to be light in your approach to work, letting go of what you don't need—discarding unnecessary psychic and physical baggage—will help. One of the traps that encumber us is the belief that we are defined by our past. What has happened before in our lives tends to govern how we deal with what is in front of us now. But this is old-model thinking. The mind will conjure up plenty of reasons why something won't work. It is fond of reciting a litany of all the failures of the past.

As long as we are confined by our previous experience, we limit our possibilities for change. Recognizing that the power of transformation lies in the present moment allows the space for creative movement. If we remain focused in the present, neither lost in the past nor projecting into the future, then it becomes possible to muster our full energies toward creativity. Such an engagement with life moves us out of an identification with our small self and into co-creation with the universe. The Chinese call it "living in the Tao." We call it being awake.

What do you actually need to manifest your best work? The answer is usually simple. Essentially, you need clarity of purpose and energy. Work is not complex. Know your purpose. Be present. Act decisively, and don't be attached to the results of the action.

Being Mindful

It is important to be mindful with our attention in the moment. The Vietnamese Buddhist teacher Thich Nhat Hanh says, "Mindfulness is the kind of energy that helps you to be really there, to live deeply each moment of your daily life. When I drink some water, I try to drink it mindfully.... Mindfulness helps you to recognize what is there. It makes life real, makes life possible."

Often when we're required to perform some task that

seems dull or menial, our mind wanders and takes us out of the here and now. Details require the practice of presence. This reminds Justine of what she often experiences while using the copy machine. She can feel her mind racing ahead, running over a list of things she has to do, or else she's mentally trying to make the machine go faster. So she put a sign over the copier for herself: "Remember to breathe and be where you are. Enjoy this moment and be grateful for your aliveness." This helps her to relax and enjoy a moment of deep breathing, a break from the fast pace of her day.

Sometimes interruptions can be an irritation to our focus, but we can, in fact, experience interruptions as a blessing. We have the blessing of our coworkers, our family, our friends. Whenever we are interrupted by a person wishing us a good morning, we can use that as a practice of mindfulness. We can choose how to be with it. Either we can be grumpy and feel that our flow has been stopped, or we can look up with a smile and see a real person smiling, caring for us since he or she is taking the time to wish us a good morning. We can allow that goodness to enter our eyes and ears and flow into our heart and all the way down to our toes, returning the smile and giving back the same goodness. It is a special moment between two human beings and should be cherished. When Justine comes to work each day she makes it a practice to walk around to each of her coworkers and say good morning. If someone is on the phone, she'll try to remember to come back later when that person has hung up. It may seem like a small thing, but she says, "This helps set the tone of my work day with my colleagues. It tells them that I'm happy to see them." If we stop to think of it, those of us who have beloved animals at home would never think of *not* saying something to our pets upon arriving after work.

A regrettable case of degenerative curmudgeonliness befell a small office we knew and worked with. One person in the office suffered from a general negative outlook. When we would call and cheerfully ask how he was doing, the very best he could say was, "So far, so good." He radiated an attitude that disaster was right around the corner. This sentiment began to infect others in the office and over time everyone retreated into their own offices, not speaking to one another unless necessary. Often when we would call, the person answering the phone would not know if anyone else was in the office or not. Eventually, it became a toxic environment where seemingly nothing could be worked out because the people became unwilling to be with one another. Although this may be an extreme case of personality irritation, we know that taking the time for the little gestures goes a long way toward keeping things pleasant even when the pressure is on.

The computer can be a fine teacher to remind us to practice mindfulness. The computer forces us to sit and do nothing while it opens up a new program. It is in this moment that the true test of presence occurs. Do we choose to relax, to use the moment to take a deep breath and feel gratefulness for our life here and now? Or do we tense against the momentary pause, allowing the stress to build? The choice is up to us—breathe and be calm, or chomp on an imaginary bit like a horse at the starting gate.

When you're not being attentive to the present moment, you may find yourself at the post office without that important letter you wanted to get in the mail before five o'clock or at a luncheon meeting in the park without your sack lunch. Whenever you lose something—a file or folder, a set of keys, a piece of paper on which mere moments ago you wrote out someone's telephone number—you can take that as a reminder that you've been out of your body and away from the present moment. Use it to bring yourself back.

Handling Details Without Expectation

Paying full attention to the seemingly least important detail is as necessary as paying full attention to the most important detail. The expression of such a commitment in your life radiates a field of energy that is attractive to others and will encourage support.

Sometimes you may be in the midst of your everyday work, daydreaming about some other creative work, and thinking, "If only this web of details were not bogging me down." The truth of the matter is that no matter what the job is, there will always be problems to contend with. All work involves some attention to minutiae; even if you get beyond the need to handle every task personally, you must *own* them in order to delegate them and have them carried out with excellence. It may help to notice the natural-world example of ants, who are highly esteemed for their careful attention to particulars. Make friends with ant energy, since each of us, like ants, must handle a superabundance of details.

The nature of our work in the world involves many activities that seem unimportant, but if they are unattended, given short shrift, or handled with less than our full focus and attention at the appropriate times, all our work is affected. In an increasingly complex world, each of us juggles many fragments simply to live and work. Handling the necessities of life, especially family life, can be a full-time occupation, as many mothers and fathers can attest.

When you can take care of the details of life and work with equanimity, without selfish motive, and without worrying or thinking about the past or future, then you are on the path to realizing your full potential. It is then that you are radiating with aliveness. The capacity to stay calmly centered amid the chaos of daily life and work is the joy we all are seeking, whether we know it or not.

Being Light and Playful

Effective work must be fun. We are convinced that life is meant to include having a good time. To the best of our knowledge, the earth is not a galactic penal colony! All our activities should include joy. No matter what, make certain that you have fun by bringing play into your work. Bringing a lightness or sense of humor to your work creates balance in the face of even the most serious challenges.

Bringing your best energy to your work creates a magnetic attraction that calls others to support the work as well. The same is true with your enthusiasm. You know how you feel when you are with someone who is lukewarm about his or her work. It's no fun, and the work itself is less effective. However, when you interact with people who are fully present and truly there the energy and enthusiasm are contagious and attractive, and you're the beneficiary.

We notice this when we go grocery shopping. There are

several large grocery stores in our town, and we find we most often go to the one where the employees seem happy. They are always smiling and joking and having a good time with their coworkers and customers. There are several other food stores where the checkers are almost always fretting about when their next break will be and about how badly they need a cup of coffee. If we ever desire to work at a grocery store, we will certainly know where to send our application.

Over the last twenty years we have spent time with a number of Tibetans and have noticed that they approach life with lightness and playfulness. Although many of them have endured great hardship, including being exiled from their native land, they're not weighed down with the pain of the experience. We've never heard one Tibetan express a negative word about the Chinese or complain about their situation. Rather, they are effusive and upbeat, continuing to look on the bright side without being unrealistic. Indeed, they are among the most pragmatic people we have ever encountered, and they are constantly breaking into laughter.

One of our favorite sayings is from the fourteenth-century Tibetan Dzogchen master Long Chen Pa, who said, "Since everything is but an apparition, perfect in being what it is, having nothing to do with good or bad, acceptance or rejection, one may well burst out in laughter."

Through our New Dimensions work we have encountered spiritual teachers from diverse traditions including Christianity, Sufism, Judaism, Islam, Hinduism, Buddhism, and others less well known. Often we have been struck by these teachers' lack of self-importance and most particularly by their sense of humor. Many possess an engaging childlike character and laugh a lot. The noted scholar, author, and philosopher Jean Houston writes, "Laughter is the loaded latency given us by nature as part of our native equipment to break up the stalemates of our lives, and urge us on to deeper and more complex forms of knowing."

Or, as Steve Bhaerman (also known as Swami Beyond-ananda) reminds us, "You can't hold any anger, you can't hold any fear, you can't hold any hurt while you're laughing."

When you're open to having fun and willing to play, you develop an ease around your work. Nothing can be too heavy or oppressive when you're able to be detached and open to what happens. When you can laugh at life's foibles as well as your own, then your work is ennobled.

FOUR

The Well of Creativity

The heart of creativity is an experience of the mystical union; the heart of the mystical union is an experience of creativity.
—JULIA CAMERON

When you do something, you should burn yourself completely, like a good bonfire, leaving no trace of yourself.
—SHUNRYU SUZUKI

The highest expression of love is creativity.
—DEEPAK CHOPRA

The more conscious you become, the more unconscious you realize you are. You don't stop. There is no stopping place. There is an openness that is part of a new style of thinking.
—PATRICIA SUN

Our actions at work can be jewels of light, illuminating our lives and expressing our own highest values.
—TARTHANG TULKU

The process of creativity has much more to do with being receptive than with actively trying to make something happen. Indeed, the more you struggle and strain, the further away you move from the creative impulse.

When creating something new, begin by gathering as much information about the project as possible. This is the "research phase." After immersing yourself thoroughly in the material, relax your mind, allowing it the freedom to go where it will. This can take hours, days, weeks — sometimes even months or years. The imagination is creating something new; when you need it, the new idea appears.

Every interview that Michael conducts taps into this process. He first has an idea of someone he wants to talk to; then he gathers all the relevant information related to that person, including any published articles or books he or she may have written. He reads any material written about them as well. He may speak with others who are familiar with the person's work. Once past the research phase, he allows a space for ideas to germinate. He does not prepare questions prior to the interview because he feels this limits the scope of the dialogue. Rather, he trusts that the questions will be there, as long as he is present and in the moment with the guest. It is amazing how often we receive correspondence from listeners saying that Michael asked exactly the question they were thinking, and how it emerged so naturally. In fact, it continues to amaze us too.

The effort and striving is in the research. The recombining of the information *is* the creative process. You don't have to think hard to be creative. Just be your natural self, and allow life to unfold. This is the creative process at work.

Original Gifts

You are an original. There is no one else on the planet exactly like you. Indeed, you are a gift to the rest of us. Not only are you to be treasured, you possess many amazing talents. In order to discover what these are, you need to pay attention to what you enjoy doing, what you're adept at, what motivates you, what brings fulfillment, and what pushes you when you're alone with yourself. The answers to these self-inquiries will guide you to know your gifts as well as your special calling. Part of your life is to develop and use these talents to make the world a better place in which to live. It is often through the work you do that your gifts are manifested.

Wasting Energy

The source of creativity lies deep inside each of us, and one of the major obstacles to manifesting it is a certain type of thinking. The constant mental struggle with conflicts, fears, and "what if" and "if only" thoughts takes up almost everyone's mental activity. The late Jiddu Krishnamurti, one of the twentieth century's greatest philosophers, raised the question of what exists when conflict is ended. "Conflict is a waste of energy. If you put gravel inside an internal combustion machine it will wear itself out. So we are wearing ourselves out psychologically. Constant conflict, struggle, never a period of quietness... [There is] never a day in which you are absolutely quiet, not occupied with something or another. If I have no conflict, I have tremendous energy. If I'm not frightened or in fear, I have tremendous energy. We are wasting our energy. If there is no wastage of energy, no conflict, then there is an *art of living,* which you don't learn in schools or colleges or from specialists."

Krishnamurti is not suggesting that we abandon thinking that is necessary to live in the world, but is saying that thinking based on worry, projection, or fear is useless. It makes our lives small, selfish, limited, and disjointed. As we're able to rid our minds of such negative thinking we become more aware and attentive, which, in his words, "is like a flame which burns out the wastage."

The Growing Edge

Each of us has a growing edge, the part of us that goes beyond what we believe to be possible. However, in daily life we develop patterns of behavior that maintain our "comfort zones" and keep us stuck in the same place. Our tendency is to want to freeze time, so that nothing changes. Of course, this is not possible, but that doesn't keep us from maintaining the same behavior. When we act this way, we stop ourselves from growing and may even regress.

We once called a friend to invite her to a small gathering with a famous dancer. We knew she was interested in dance, but when we called she said, "Oh, no, I couldn't go. It's on Tuesday, and I always go to the movies on Tuesday night." We were surprised that she turned down this chance simply because she didn't want to change her routine. It would be good to remember that practicing spontaneity stimulates the creative process. When we change a pattern it allows the energy to flow. You never know when opportunity may come knocking at your door. You must be willing to open it wide.

Each of us has certain routines we perform every day, from the way we brush our teeth to the way we enter a grocery store. You may wet your toothbrush first and then turn off the water, or you may leave the water running. You may be in the habit of going to the produce section first or heading straight for the paper goods. It's easy to establish these patterns; they make you feel safe and the world more familiar. But when you adopt them, you give up your conscious, decision-making activity and move into what we call "automatic pilot" or a habitual groove. If you are to call upon your innate creative abilities, you must wake yourself up from the slumber of routine. Small changes will send a message to your body to pay attention, to expect the unexpected. You must examine yourself for ways you can change your habits. The most effective means of breaking through "stuck behavior" is to let go and practice spontaneity. Be in the present and don't plan so much.

Years ago we lived in a duplex townhouse. One day our neighbor said to us, "I can't figure you guys out; you have no discernible patterns." We took this as a compliment, although we're not sure he meant it in that way. The fact is you will never know the future and the sense of control is merely an illusion, so it is better to act freely in the moment with trust in life's magic. It's not easy to do this. It requires practice, but the rewards can be extraordinary.

Try entering the grocery store through another door and going to a different aisle first. Pick up the phone with your other hand and listen with the opposite ear from the one you're used to listening with. Most of all, stay open to opportunities that are coming your way. You will discover aspects of yourself you never knew were there and you will accomplish things you never thought possible.

The Tao of Work

Taking care of what is necessary and doing what needs to be done without distraction are essential. Attend to the work without wasting energy through negative mind chatter. Be deliberate in your actions. Make certain that you've taken care of your responsibilities so that you are like a freshly turned field, ready for seeds to grow. There's a mystery here. A new flow often emerges in its own time, and it's up to you to be open and able to move with it when the time is right. The way of the artist is not something to be controlled. What you *can* do is imagine the space within yourself to allow the energy to flourish and be available for whatever you are doing.

Many young people are very good at allowing the flow to happen. This is not because of their youth or some special past karma, but rather because they are not so entrenched in negative thinking such as worry, fear, and conflict. There is more energy available to them because they are not concerned about maintaining a roof over their heads and putting food on the table. It's always a good practice to look regularly at what you've committed to in the form of responsibilities that cause you to worry. Young people seem to have more energy to learn a musical instrument, develop a skill in sports, or learn a language than those in their thirties and beyond. How often have you said, "I wish I'd learned that when I was younger and had the time and energy"? As Krishnamurti says, "Transformation is not in the future, can never be in the future. It can only be in the now, from moment to moment." Don't wait for some imaginary future when things will be better. Do it now.

You possess the capacity to be original, to express yourself as yourself. This capacity is enhanced by practice. If it is music you love and you want to play the violin, you must master various techniques in order to do justice to the instrument and fully express yourself. You may have exclaimed over someone else's efforts, "Oh, you're so artistic, I could never do something like that." But you probably could, if you put in the time to practice your art. The inverse of the law of supply-side economics applies here: By tapping into your inventive source and practicing your unique expression, you can have more energy, not less.

The muse needs to feel welcome. You must be a good host and invite her in as an honored guest. When you have friends over for a meal, you clean the house and plan a menu of delicious food. You look forward to the camaraderie and good fellowship. You take a break from the list of concerns and conflicts that is almost constantly running in your head. This is exactly what you must do for the creative imagination to soar. Set a table for her; lay before her a feast that is inviting, a virtual cornucopia.

Mind-Body Connection

Intelligence means more than the intellect or what we know in our brains. Creative intelligence includes both the intellect and the imagination. Knowing goes beyond the mind-brain

and includes the intelligence inherent within human consciousness. Part of learning to be inventive is to let go of
thinking so much. This is not an intellectual process. It is an
energetic process. Letting go of our thoughts and releasing
our desire to control reality allows the inspiration to emerge.
When we find ourselves engaged in the fire of birthing
something new, we're not thinking. We're actively in the
moment, living and expressing our passion. It's a unification
experience, when our thoughts, feelings, actions, and words
are as one entity without conflict. We're not thinking one
thing, feeling another, doing something else, and saying a
fourth thing, as so often can be the case in this world of busy-
ness. This is why meditation and solitude can be catalysts for
originality. They afford you the opportunity to slow the pace
of life and reflect in silence without external distraction.

Thinking often transforms into worry, and worry is
fertile ground for more worry. When Justine starts thinking
and worrying too much, she uses a technique that she's
developed to clear her crowded brain.

While sitting comfortably, take a deep breath. As you
fill your lungs with oxygen, raise your shoulders to your
ears. As you exhale, release your shoulders, allowing them to
drop. Then take three controlled breaths—hold the air for a
moment after you inhale and allow a brief moment of no air
in your lungs after you exhale. On each out-breath use your
diaphragm to force the air out of your lungs. Push really hard
to get as much air out of the lungs as possible and hold a
moment before inhaling. Then relax your diaphragm, which
allows the lungs to fill up with air quite naturally on the in-
breath. After the three breaths, allow your breathing to be

natural and easy. Closing your eyes, imagine all your thoughts and worries as little stones that are held tightly in your two fists. Then slowly open your fists and imagine that each of these stones has turned into a golden yellow butterfly; see them as fluttering from your open hands, transforming the tangled mess in your head into light as they fly away.

This is an exercise that can be used wherever you are, driving a car (without closing your eyes!), sitting at your desk, or waiting in line. Justine has found it useful because it brings her back into her body. By relaxing the body and feeding oxygen to the brain, the litany of thought is interrupted and peace is possible. Do not underestimate this practice. We have found that it elevates us out of the mundane and into the limitless field of possibilities.

Many of us have not yet developed an ear for listening to our bodies even though they speak to us all the time. We need to trust our instincts. We are more than our thinking brain. There is much intelligence in the body, and we need to include it in our awareness of the symphony we truly are. Justine has an example of how we often don't listen.

One brisk morning, Justine was walking Mogan, a feisty Arabian gelding, around the ring. She could feel he was looking for an excuse to cut up. The morning was cold and he was full of bounce. Coming toward them was a squirrel, scampering down the fence. Mogan had not yet seen it. Justine could feel her body instinctively wanting to turn the horse around and walk the other way before he caught sight of the squirrel. However, for some reason she let her mind-brain prevail and did not act on this impulse. When Mogan saw the squirrel, he took an enormous leap to the side and almost dropped Justine on the hard ground. Afterward Justine wondered why she hadn't followed her own body knowledge. She was shaken by the close call. It would have been such a simple thing to turn the horse around and avoid the possibility of getting injured in a fall.

As a first step, you must look for some simple movement that is close to you, one your body already knows how to do, *and then do it*—metaphorically turn your horse around. Take that first step, and the others will follow.

Teacher Brooke Medicine Eagle shares a technique she learned for getting down into our bodies. Most of us are very adept at being up and away in our heads and not down in our bellies.

Find a "belly rock," a smooth, rounded river rock that would feel good lying on your belly. Make sure it is hefty enough to feel, although you don't want to be uncomfortable under its weight. Lie down and place the rock about two fingers below your navel. Breathe down into your belly and become aware of the rock. If your mind wanders, gently bring your attention back to the weight of the stone on your belly. Do this for five minutes. Brooke tells us, "Over time, as you practice this, you will begin to develop a more mystical sense of your connection with the Earth on which we all live. The image I was given was that I am connected to Mother Earth through an invisible umbilical cord and she feeds me information and connection and love and nurturance through that. And as I am connected so we are all connected to the Earth and all things, the animals, the trees, the birds. That's where we feel, understand, hear, and get the news of life. Getting down into our belly literally helps us feel and understand and know that connection and not just think about it."

Taking Retreats

It's important to remove yourself occasionally from your everyday environment and take time to *be* rather than *do*. Whenever we have taken time to go on retreat, we notice that afterward our work is affected in a direct and positive way.

There are many opportunities and places available to go on retreat. Sometimes we'll attend a meditation retreat together. Other times Michael will go alone to a Trappist abbey or Justine will go to the desert. Such a departure from the daily routine of work and life can serve as a restorative to the spirit and the soul. A retreat into nature can rejuvenate. Recently Justine took a whitewater rafting trip with her women's group. "I felt totally refreshed," she reports. "I went from the small-muscle movements of my everyday work to the large-muscle movements required in paddling. I also tried my hand at the long oars, which felt as deeply satisfying to my soul as any meditation retreat I've ever attended." A new perspective will arise simply from changing your surroundings for several days. The spiritual focus enables you to reconnect with the deep source of your creative power in a positive way. It also reminds you that life includes more than work, no matter how personally self-satisfying and rewarding it may be.

In our place of work, taking a mini-retreat is encouraged by using what we call "well days." Each staff person gets four "well days" per year. These are meant to be used for supporting and restoring your creative energy flow. "Well days" are in addition to the traditional sick leave. They are intended to be used. They are not cumulative.

Practice Solitude

Just as retreats renew your soul's purpose, it's also important to have some solitude in your daily life, if only in the early morning when you awaken and have not yet entered the day. Finding moments during the day when you can separate from the pace and be alone for a few minutes can also be immensely satisfying and help you return to your work feeling fresh and recharged.

If it's possible to go outside into nature, so much the better. Nature has a restorative quality that is palpable. Feeling our connection to the living Earth—the trees, the rocks, the birds, the biosphere of which we're an integral part—can reconnect us with the largeness of life unfolding all around and through us. We lose contact with this reality as we tap away on our computers, under artificial lights, amidst the constant buzzing and ringing of telephones, doorbells, message beepers, fax machines, and intercoms.

Taking a "nature break" can inspire us to address our work and obligations with renewed vigor and energy. There is an inner peace that comes from communing with the natural world. Even in the midst of the city there are plenty of places to sit and gaze at the sky or watch the pigeons parading around in their iridescent feathered coats.

A man who attended one of our seminars told us that when he was living in a high-rise apartment building in a major city, his need for something natural and growing was so great that he made a shallow, waterproof box about six feet long and three feet wide, placed it near a big window, and rolled out a strip of sod inside it. He created his own patch of grass in his apartment and walked barefoot on it at least once a day. He would water it and cut it, filling the room with the special smell of newly cut grass.

Recently Justine went swimming with some women friends in a pond several miles north of our home. "I'd been working steadily at the computer day after day for weeks. So when an invitation came for an outing, I couldn't resist. The pond turned out to be quite large. So large, in fact, that it took about half an hour to swim from one end of it to the other. I would close my eyes and feel the warm and gentle rays of the early morning sun on my lids. I realized that my body was starving for this natural light and my eyes were hungry for the sight of the rolling, golden hills that surrounded the pond. The curves and roundness of the natural world were such a contrast to the straight lines of my desk and my office. An impressive blue heron gave us a blessing by flying over our heads. Later, in a frustrating moment at my desk as I was waiting for a technician to pick up my call about some computer glitch, the blue heron revisited me in my mind's eye, and my body relaxed. The morning swim continues to work its magic on my day. It reminded me of a haiku poem I once wrote:

> *Waves pounding shore — phsssssssh*
> *Beneath, in ocean stillness*
> *Whale glides — no effort."*

Inspiration

Creative energy is at the heart of the universe, and this energy is available to you at all times. Draw on it, trust it, use it, let it move you toward your own deep mastery. Rely on your inspiration no matter what.

Inspiration comes from the inner depths and carries the message and energy of spirit. In French the word *inspiration* means "breathing in." It comes from the Latin *in spiritus,* which is "in the spirit" or "of the spirit." Take a deep breath and let your own creative spirit come through you. Inspiration often occurs outside the context of the workplace itself. It's useful to have a small notebook or a tape recorder in order to record your insights when they occur. Michael finds airplane travel or long car drives to be especially inspiring environments. Justine often receives new ideas through dreams. Frequently, after we have spent considerable time and energy exploring a problem, we'll release it and stop thinking about it for a while. Then, perhaps days or weeks later, a solution will appear, as if by magic. Logic and rationality are important elements in the germinal process but can get in the way of inspiration, which is mysterious and moves to a different drummer. New ideas are often at odds with existing logic. It is necessary to suspend the old belief systems to allow new ideas and new logic in. Letting go of what we think we know can be an invitation to inspiration.

Justine had a crash course in this "stop thinking about the problem" technique early on in our relationship. Shortly after we got together we decided to travel throughout the United States and Mexico for a year in a camper. Because

Robert, her nine-year-old son, would be accompanying us, she became very worried about his schooling. He was in the third grade and she didn't want him to lose a year of school. Justine had been a grade-school teacher and her concerns were based on her experience of the public school system. To make sure Robert would not miss a beat, she got her California teacher's certificate and collected all the textbooks from a local school so she could tutor him. We began the trip and for three months we traveled without an itinerary. It was glorious except when it came time for the tutoring sessions. They were hell. Robert hated them, and she hated them. She fretted and asked Michael to help her figure out what to do. He kept saying, "Don't worry, it will work out." She kept asking, "Yes, but how?"

What she was unable to do during that trip was stop worrying about Robert's "education." However, Robert was receiving a priceless bounty of creative stimulation. He was learning far beyond anything that could be found in a third-grade reader, but Justine wasn't of a mind to see that at the time. She sees it now, as does Robert. That incident remains the high-water mark for her. Now, when she feels herself beginning to fret in much the same way, she recalls how everything turned out so beautifully on that trip so many years ago.

Dreams and Visions

Acting on your most deeply felt aspirations may not make life convenient. In fact, it will often have quite the opposite effect and upset your proverbial applecart. As you follow this calling your life will become intertwined with others. You will meet people you never dreamed of meeting and find yourself motivated to develop a host of new skills. This is the beauty of it. In our work, we find that we so love the people with whom we are working, it feels as though the product of our work is just the excuse for us to "play" together and to learn new ways of living and being.

Creativity can be a messy process, just like when we were little kids playing in the dirt. Dry dirt was never as much fun as adding a little water, and then more water, until we had a wonderful mud puddle in which we could build towers and castles with moats where alligators swam. So allow yourself to get dirty. Your rational, reasoning mind is only part of the equation. It's the part that wants to keep clean and neat. Give yourself the freedom to splash in the mud of your creative dreams. Writer Brenda Ueland advises, "Imagination needs moodling—long, inefficient, happy idling, dawdling and puttering."

To hold your longings is to carry the seeds of your creativity, which, when nurtured, will manifest your dreams as actual events. Shakespeare wrote, "In dreams begin our possibilities." During the early years of our work Michael held the dream that the *New Dimensions* radio series would eventually be heard all over the United States. At first the idea seemed daunting because of all the work involved. For the first six years we were heard exclusively in the San Francisco Bay area. Some of us became extremely doubtful that we would be able to manifest that dream, especially when our main station canceled the live four-hour program that had been airing weekly for five years. There was little financial support and our listening audience was literally eliminated overnight.

Nevertheless, Michael held on to the dream, and then the public broadcasting satellite came into being. We received a private gift to finance promoting the program series to public radio and a foundation grant to finance the satellite distribution of the program. Within a few months, more than a hundred radio stations agreed to carry the program for at least one year. But it was only because the dream was kept alive that we were ready to make it happen when the opportunity arose. Since then we have nurtured the national outreach of our radio work to more than three hundred radio stations, which now carry the weekly *New Dimensions* series. In 1988 New Dimensions Radio began broadcasting worldwide via shortwave and is now heard in more than 130 countries. It is also broadcast globally via the U.S. Armed Forces Radio Network, as well as by C-band to owners of large satellite dishes and on the Internet via the New Dimensions website.

There's something mysterious and powerful about holding a vision. It's like joining forces with the creative power of the universe. The willingness to act on your deepest impulses serves as a clarion call to attract support. Once you have jumped over the line of indecision, doubt, and worry about the outcome, then the release of the energy necessary to wrestle with these barriers to creative action will begin to make the vision real.

FIVE

Working Through the Wilderness

You may be disappointed if you fail, but you are doomed if you don't try.
—BEVERLY SILLS

I worry no matter how cynical you become, it's never enough to keep up.
—JANE WAGNER

Life shrinks or expands in proportion to one's courage.
—ANAIS NIN

In the middle of difficulty lies opportunity.
—ALBERT EINSTEIN

Anxiety is fuel. We can use it to write with, paint with, work with.
—JULIA CAMERON

It's a funny thing about life; if you refuse to accept anything but the best, you very often get it.
—SOMERSET MAUGHAM

Approaching life as a playground instead of a battleground can have an enormous impact upon the quality and outcome of your actions. Joseph Campbell spoke to this point: "Work begins when you don't like what you're doing. There's a wise saying—make your hobby your source of income. Then there's no such thing as work, and there's no such thing as getting tired. That's been my experience. I did just what I wanted to do. It takes courage at first, because who the hell wants you to do just what you want to do? They've all got a lot of plans for you. But you can make it happen.

"I think it's very important for young people to have the courage to do what seems to them significant in their life, and not just take a job in order to make money. This takes a bit of prudence and very careful planning, and may delay financial achievement and comfortable living. But the ultimate result will be very much to their pleasure."

Another key to effective work is to release negative attitudes you may be carrying. Cynicism is rampant in our society. Many take the position that with the monumental problems we face, the only intelligent attitude is one of pessimism. Their idea is that you're not seeing reality correctly if you're hopeful, or that your optimistic view of the situation is neither realistic nor rational. Yet it is clear that cynicism and negativity can have a destructive effect on your capacity to live creatively. Pessimism closes you off from what we call "possibility thinking." In possibility thinking, no matter what the situation, there are always many ways in which to view it, each one providing a different avenue for addressing the particular concern. When your thinking does not become muscle-bound by negativity, more energy and possibilities are available to you.

Pessimism robs you of energy. It disempowers you and blocks you from fulfilling your purpose. Optimism, on the other hand, allows you full access to your power. You can make a difference, beginning with yourself. You are the master of your destiny, not a victim of external circumstances. How can you *not* be hopeful and optimistic? You're alive. You're breathing. Life is a gift, and you possess it. Being cynical is a form of dying, not living.

Not the least of the arguments for a positive attitude is that it's more healthy to be optimistic. Bernie Siegel, M.D., who has worked extensively with cancer patients, says, "I'm not an optimist, I'm a realist.... Life is tough, but since I'm here for a limited time, I choose joy. That's the choice that we all have to make, or we're not going to be grateful for life, or be happy."

In 1989 we attended a conference in Costa Rica called "Seeking the True Meaning of Peace." The highlight of that event was the presence of the Dalai Lama, the exiled religious leader of Tibet. Someone in the audience asked him why he seemed so happy all the time, why he kept working on behalf of Tibet when there was so little hope that the Chinese government would ever consent to leaving it. It appeared there was no way that he would be able to return to Tibet and peacefully lead his people.

The Dalai Lama responded with simplicity and power. He said he chose not to be pessimistic because that made him feel bad. It was better to arise in the morning feeling good, and he felt better when he was optimistic. He went on to say that he didn't know what the outcome of his work on behalf of the Tibetan people would be. Their situation might get better or it might not. He didn't know the future. However, he did what he did because it was the right and good thing for him to do—not because it might work out to a positive conclusion. It made him feel good to do what he felt was "right action."

Justine recalls listening to him speak. In that moment she knew that she had been hedging her bets, which kept her from acting with her full and positive energies on what she knew to be right and good. She then decided to go for what she believed to be right and good, no matter what. She hasn't been able to turn her entrenched habits of negative thinking around overnight, but she's making progress, and she keeps at it.

It feels better to see with positive eyes. It gives you more energy to act in positive ways to influence the future.

Difficulties and Problems as Energizers

Sometimes people think that once they have discovered their purpose in life or found their passion, then all will be well and their problems will disappear. Well, perhaps some problems will no longer exist, but following your life's path as a spiritual practice is a difficult journey, fraught with challenges. Bucky Fuller used to say, "Humans are here as local problem-solvers in the Universe," and that as we develop the ability to solve problems, the problems become bigger. He could be right, judging from the size of some of the difficulties we face in the world today.

Futurist Barbara Marx Hubbard sees these global challenges as "evolutionary pile-drivers" that push us to greater problem-solving. Even as a forest fire wreaks destruction, it also catalyzes new life in that some seeds germinate only as a result of the high temperatures brought by fire. The obstacle you encounter is also the opportunity for something new, because it forces you to go deeper and discover previously hidden resources. Like fine steel, you are tempered by the fires of life. This leads to asking new questions and extending the boundaries of what is possible.

We can't tell you how often we have seen a business, idea, or service fail simply because the person or persons involved did not have the willingness to weather the difficulties. The obstacles that emerge are there to help you refine and clarify your purpose, so that you become more effective. See the obstacle as another opportunity to help you get better at what you do. Jungian analyst June Singer says, "When things are not working for us, instead of fighting and struggling, we need to say, 'What's happening here? How am I not being true to who I am? What is pulling me away from my purpose?' "

Making Mistakes

Look for the value in what you are doing, whatever it may be, and be flexible. Realize that making mistakes is part of the creative process, and be grateful for what you learn because of them. Don't succumb to conventional wisdom and fall into the trap of the "can't or won't" syndrome. Remember that when someone says *you can't*, usually it means that *they didn't*. Realize that you are the only *you* on the planet and you are meant to express your gifts, no matter what.

One of the most important lessons we learned from

Buckminster Fuller was that to make mistakes is the way we learn how life works. In order to make mistakes, of course, you have to *do* something. Taking action is what creates results. If you don't move toward your dream, then you will never realize it.

All of us have been conditioned through schooling to believe that making mistakes is wrong. We received a failing grade for the wrong answer, so we spend the rest of our lives trying to avoid mistakes at all costs. And we pay for this with our fire and our creativity. We want to "play it safe," so we never learn what we need to know. Thomas Edison's retort to someone's query about the large number of experiments he conducted in order to invent the electric light bulb was that he had *successfully learned* a few thousand ways it *didn't* work.

You can choose to see the foul-ups as teachers. Do you learn from them or do you blame the teacher? The teacher could be a late check or a missed appointment. Do you feel joy and continue to live your zeal, or do you feel miserable and stuck, unable to do anything?

Errors show us the way to go forward. They tell us what we need to learn, and show us what we must study in order to attain our dream. There's no doubt that if we act, we're going to do some things wrong. But another opportunity will appear, and we can do better the next time. Doing something is what's important.

Asking New Questions

The Reverend Mary Manin Morrissey gives us three magic words that free us from our limiting attitudes. She says,

"There is a very simple phrase that you can use to help you open up to a new mind: 'Up until now.' Those three little words become a very powerful changing point in anyone's life. If we take a look at our dream and our mind wants to think, 'I can't possibly do that,' we can say, 'Up until now I haven't been able to go to school. Up until now I haven't been able to break free financially.'

"'Up until now' frees us into a new level of thinking from which new possibilities can occur. Einstein said, 'Significant problems we face in life cannot be solved at the level of thinking that created those problems.' Well, that says to us that there is another level of thinking available, beyond the level of thinking that creates the problems we're experiencing. 'Up until now' frees us to that new level."

When we have a staff meeting we often help one another by using this phrase as we talk about new ways of working together. This is done in good humor and with excellent results. These words, "up until now," take care of two major concerns. They acknowledge that until now things have been one way and it is important to speak out loud about how it's been in the past, for that shines a light in dark corners. These three words allow us a place from which to start afresh.

Overcoming Worry and Negativity

Although it is your natural tendency to be creative (truly it is!), you may notice that many of your days are filled with distractions and activities that prevent you from feeling your innate inventiveness. The question is, how do we arrive at a place of inner calm when we are feeling totally overwhelmed by negativity and worry?

If you are feeling listless, bored, or even angry about your work, ask yourself why you are doing what you're doing. Is your motivation outer-directed—are you doing your work in order to receive approval from others? Or perhaps you are working for the money to pay off debts and feed a family.

Sometimes it is worthwhile to step back. For example, you may be working at something you love—at least you can remember that you loved it when you started doing it. But lately it's been a drag and a drain. All the details have piled up, you are on edge with your coworkers, and the fun and excitement you used to feel is just not there. This is the time to stop, sit back, and breathe. Notice what is really bugging you. Ask yourself, "Am I in the future? Am I in the past?" When you are feeling like this, bring yourself into the moment. Don't allow your thoughts to carry you away, like riding a wild horse off into the wilderness of your mind, instead of being where you are. It's not about getting somewhere. It's about living life, now, here in this moment.

Barbara Sher, career counselor and author of *I Could Do Anything If I Only Knew What It Was*, talks about subsidizing your passion: "You need financial safety and you need some modicum of health. But they've studied happiness, and found out that once you're not in a state of terror about money, it doesn't matter how much money you have. [Quantity of money] is not related to happiness at all.

"There are two kinds of jobs in this world. One is the toxic job—it poisons you, and eats up all your time. This is a bad job. Whether you are going after a dream or not you've got to get rid of it or change it. You can't do that to yourself; life is too short.

"The other kind of job is known as 'not bad, but just not enough.' That's a good job. When you have a job that is not enough, you don't have to subtract the job, you just *add your dream to it*. So this job should never make you work more than eight hours a day, preferably less. Never more than five days a week, preferably less. It should have pleasant people who tell good jokes at the water cooler, and hopefully hospitalization insurance. That's what you need; then you can call that job a subsidy to the arts."

What Sher means is that it is possible to follow your passion in addition to the job you now hold. In other words, it's not either the job *or* your passion. It can be both. This certainly was the case with us. For years Michael earned income from other sources by using his various talents and expertise while still pursuing his true purpose at every opportunity. It was a necessity. He did seminars on communications techniques for nonprofit organizations; he has been a marketing and fund-raising consultant to various socially responsible organizations; he has served as an acquisitions editor for book publishers; he has presented other seminars and workshops related to living your vision, work as spiritual practice, and right living. These jobs not only provided income that enabled him to continue to pursue his main passion, but taught him new skills, which he brought to the work of New Dimensions.

Joseph Campbell once asked a provocative question that is relevant to challenging work situations: "Is the system going to flatten you out and deny your humanity, or are you going to be able to make use of the system to the attainment of human purposes?"

We know of a person who works for a large company that is well-respected in its field. It happens that the founder and chief executive is an autocratic tyrant whose business has been successful in spite of his leadership. The service the company provides is much desired and is largely facilitated by people such as our friend, who works away from the main office. This factor is perhaps the saving grace for him because even though he is rated one of the best of all the employees in what he does, he does not receive acknowledgment and is often critiqued unfairly by the chief executive. However, our friend has created his job in such a way that he is mostly outside of the dysfunctional office environment; he lives with his family in a beautiful rural area away from the pressures of the urban sprawl; he devotes considerable time to his family and does receive positive feedback and gratitude from those he directly serves as well as through a large circle of good friends unrelated to his work.

Reflecting on what he has accomplished, including maintaining a happy marriage and, together with his wife, raising two sons and a daughter into adulthood, he is wealthy in relationships and personal fulfillment. He has also been able to pursue his love of poetry and has had several volumes of his poetry published. This has been achieved in spite of working for a boss who does not appreciate his talents. How? He let go of expecting acknowledgment from his supervisor and received it elsewhere. He found meaning directly in the work he was doing through serving others and through his poetry. He chose a supportive living environment and made his family and children a priority. He created a support circle of friends who could help through difficult times and who encouraged his creativity.

Small worries and aggravations are part of life. Just as we put out one brush fire another starts up. We've mentioned many ways in which to deal with these eddies in the flow of our daily life, such as focusing on the breath, taking a walk, humor, and so on. But what about the big worries that can rumble down low in your gut, such as "How will I pay the rent or mortgage next week?" Some worries don't involve a roof over the head, health, or food on the table, but we feel as if we will be obliterated if we don't solve them—they seemingly have no solutions. On occasion, Justine wakes up early, before dawn has broken. She calls this time, with the night still lingering, the time of the wolf—a waiting, watching time when all her fears seem to flood her consciousness and she feels powerless to take action. Her inner confidence is low in those moments, and the obstacles loom like gargoyles perched on a fortress wall, ready to swoop down and do harm to her.

Michael has invented a set of questions that help during these low periods. "Are you hungry right now? Are you cold? Is there a roof over your head?" When Justine answers, "No, I am not cold or hungry, and yes, there is a roof over my head," Michael will say, "Then what's the worry? Starvation is not upon us—we have our aliveness." He'll ask, "What is the worst thing that can happen?" She replies, "To fall out of the universe." One thing of which we are both confident, no matter what, is that we can't fall out of the universe—we are always home.

These questions help Justine to switch channels, just like on a television set, from her worried-about-the-future channel to the I-can't-fall-out-of-the-universe channel. One channel broadcasts never-ending soap operas with multiple tales of woe. The other channel is a combination of Carl Sagan's *Cosmos* and the Discovery Channel, where everything is in its proper place, moving with perfect rhythm.

Something sacred in the center of each of us is not touched by fear and worry. This is where the soul resides. We find the way Tibetans describe different realities useful. They use the terms *relative* and *absolute*.

In our practice of those concepts, the relative level is right here, in our face with the full force of emotion, upset, joy, and sorrow. The absolute level is beyond duality; neither love nor hate exists there. There is neither attraction nor aversion in the absolute. All is perfect just as it is. This is also true on the relative level, but we're often not able to perceive it that way. We find it very helpful to apply this concept in our daily lives, especially when we are in the grip of wanting to change things beyond our control.

You can be assured that your sacred center can never be hurt or touched by the foul weather of your emotions. Your inner core of clarity and flow in the universe is as bright and shining as the sun and is never, ever sullied by local, emotional weather. It is just that way.

Sogyal Rinpoche, author of *The Tibetan Book of Living and Dying,* often uses the spaciousness of the sky to convey the possibilities of the unclouded mind. Imagine waking up on the morning you're to leave on a long trip and finding gray skies and drizzling rain. The wet streets reflect the dreary skies. You get on the plane, and as it takes off, you watch the wings cut through the dark clouds as you are bounced upward. Suddenly you burst into light so blinding you need your sunglasses. You had forgotten all about the sun. But here it is, unaffected by the weather below.

This is how it is with us. Our personal weather overcomes us and our projects overwhelm us. We get fixated on the blocks. We procrastinate. There are many things we do (or don't do) that exacerbate our agitation.

In the early 1970s Justine was backpacking in the mountains with her son, Robert, who was then seven. He was tired, hot, and not a little frustrated. At one point he came to a smooth rock in the middle of the trail. The rock was about eighteen inches long by twelve inches wide, and was tilted at a 30-degree angle to the trail. It was covered by fine pumice stone dust, which made it extremely slippery. Robert stepped on it, and immediately his foot slid down. He stepped again with the same results. In his upset, he became fixated on the rock and flung himself on it with both feet, trying to get beyond it by running on its surface. The obvious solution was to step around the rock. But he would have none of that and soon exhausted himself.

When we come to that slippery rock in our work, rather than butting up against it and wearing ourselves out, let us stop and see what we can do to shift the energy. Take a deep breath. Say a prayer. Think about something wonderful. Then step over the rock!

Transforming Toxic Work

If your work is problematic and toxic, then you may want to look for something else that is not destructive to your being. When you find yourself in a work situation in which you're unable to thrive in the overall climate, ask yourself, "Is this work situation toxic to my being? Is it a work situation that is overwhelmingly negative? Do I have to cut myself off from others to get my work done? Is the pressure of the job requiring me to give up what makes life enjoyable?" If you answer yes to these questions, then you need to take another look at the perceived benefits of that job and ask yourself if they truly enhance your life and well-being.

We know a woman who was getting a generous salary working for a service organization that sought to preserve forested land from exploitive development. This is fine and necessary work. The glitch was that her employer, the founder of the organization, was a tyrant in the workplace. There was no joy in the work. The woman had several meetings with her employer about the stresses she was experiencing, and she tried to stick with it, but after about a year she decided the pay and the good cause were not worth the personal pain of working there. She placed the quality of her life first. Now she works for herself out of her home. She has more quality time with her three children and has found interesting and fulfilling work as well. She took the leap and was met with a resounding yes from the universe.

Sometimes events are beyond your control, such as corporate decisions to merge, sell, or downsize. You may find yourself in an overwrought work environment with people who are stressed out and unpleasant to work with. Corporations are like people, always in motion: growing, dying, expanding, contracting. All this motion causes fear and tension. When large events happen, such as a merger or the arrival of a new company president, everyone in the workplace is affected. Even though these changes are not within your realm of control, you can choose how to respond to them. If seeking other employment is not possible, then there are ways to detoxify the situation so that your work becomes more meaningful and self-fulfilling. This is not an easy task. It may be simple, but it is not easy.

All work, whether it is ideal or not, will require you to put your spiritual and psychological skills into practice. When work involves interactions with others, then we will be challenged to live the most basic of spiritual principles we have learned, such as kindness, patience, prudence, truthfulness, perseverance, and humility. Even if your work situation is the best of the best, all these principles must be brought to bear in our everyday contacts. Often it is through sharing painful situations with others that we attain deeper levels of emotional and spiritual maturity. You may notice how your life has blossomed with greater confidence because you've dealt successfully with difficulties.

Denial will not make the problems go away, but it is often the common reaction to knotty work scenes. You may tell yourself that you prefer to let things lie and do nothing, hoping they will go away. This may be a good choice. But if doing nothing adds to your stress, tension, and feelings of oppression or isolation, then you must take steps to transform the experience. It is natural to feel upset and even angry, but don't get stuck in "victim" consciousness. Remember the ancient Chinese proverb "Be not afraid of growing slowly; be afraid only of standing still."

Our friend Nita came to work with New Dimensions after experiencing burnout at a large corporation. In her former job, she had suffered through a high-pressure institutional situation where the atmosphere was very impersonal and the bottom line was to get the product out at all costs. This scene only exacerbated her already low self-esteem. Rather than stay and feel powerless to change her situation, she left the company. She worked with us for about a year but, as a single mother of two sons, found that she needed more money and decided to go back to her old employer. However, during her time away from the large company, she had learned to pay attention to the smallest details. One of the skills she concentrated on was her writing. She was an atrocious speller, and had always thought that being a good speller was beyond her reach. One day she made up her mind that she was going to be an excellent speller. She obtained a good dictionary and thesaurus and taught herself to be careful with every letter and report she put out. After about six months, her manager acknowledged her good reports. Others started noticing her attention to detail, and before long she was given a 12 percent raise and promoted to a managerial job. She began receiving more positive feedback on her work and has become a super manager.

What Nita did was to go back into her old job with new enthusiasm. She was not a meek lamb going to the slaughter, but a warrior taking charge of what was in her domain of influence.

Justine recalls a time in her own life when she was especially agitated with a certain colleague at work. She felt paranoid and misunderstood by this coworker. She sat down to write a letter in order to express her deep feelings, and just before E-mailing the letter, she paused for a few minutes and tried out an exercise suggested by Neale Donald Walsch, author of *Conversations with God*. His advice when confronting a problematic situation is to ask the question "What would love do now?" When we are in the middle of our upset and want to blame someone, anyone but ourselves, it is very difficult to reach for our higher state of consciousness. It is tough to stop in the middle of our muddle and ask, "What is the Christian or Buddhist action required here?" But when we say, "What would love do now?," it seems less fraught with the moralistic, "thou shalt" or "thou shalt not." Love resides in an uncomplicated place, one that is felt in the center of the body, in the heart, bypassing the mind. Each of us knows that place.

Before sending her message, Justine made a prayer to help love express itself through her and into the E-mail. After a few minutes her fingers tapped out on the keyboard the perfect words in a revised edition of her note. This time she was able to communicate with equanimity from the fullness of her being. Her communication was well received, and a situation that could have escalated was defused and transformed.

No matter how burdensome the work, you can find a way through the briar patch by adjusting your attitude. A shift in perspective can expand your awareness and open you to new possibilities. When your horizon broadens, new vistas appear. Additionally, here is a list of reminders to help you stay in the creative flow even in the midst of the most troublesome work scene.

TWELVE WAYS TO BE CREATIVE
IN A TOXIC WORKPLACE

- ◆ Let go of wanting approval from authority figures.
- ◆ Look for meaning in the ordinary things.

- Do not compare yourself with others.

- Give up self-judgment.

- Find activities outside of work that provide satisfaction and fulfillment.

- Perceive obstacles and problems as opportunities to grow and deepen your experience of life.

- Stay in the present so as to avoid worry and doubt.

- Detach yourself from expectations.

- Do not submit passively, but surrender yourself totally to the work that needs doing.

- Pay attention, don't think too much, and stay light on your feet.

- Be positive and hopeful.

- Don't take anything personally.

Overcoming Resistance

The broadcast work that we do requires an enormous amount of detail. The taping of an interview takes far less time and energy than arranging it and getting it on the air. So if we're unable to handle the mundane aspects of our work, we'll never be able to reach completion.

It's all one piece, and all of it is creative. Some parts of it are more fun than others, and it's only natural to want more of the fun. Also, it is far easier to remain with what we know how to do, what we are "good" at doing. Learning new skills feels uncomfortable, so we stay with what feels comfortable. We may not even know what we are best at, because we keep working only with what we are good at. In the book *First Things First*, Steven Covey points out, "Decisions are easier when it's a question of 'good' or 'bad.' We can easily see how some ways we could spend our time are wasteful, mind-numbing, even destructive. But for most of us, the issue is not between the 'good' and the 'bad,' but between the 'good' and the 'best.' So often, the enemy of the best is the good. Only focus on your best, not what you are good at, otherwise you'll never get to your best."

To live our dreams, we need to wake up. Waking up challenges the place of snugness inside all of us where we escape the vicissitudes of life. Anything new and different will be challenging, so we must learn to be at ease with the discomfort. If our actions are driven by a larger sense of purpose, then the discomfort can be acceptable. However, if there is a lack of meaning, then it's difficult, if not impossible, to reconcile the dis-ease.

Conscious Choice

Pay attention to what you are feeling. Notice your personal energy flow. In today's fast-paced world, it's easy to become vulnerable to external pressures and lose your natural sensitivity to your inner process. Recently when the New Dimensions tape order person, Debbie Pollock, was feeling overwhelmed by the task at hand, she was advised to think of it as a game. With quick wit she retorted, "Well, if it's a game, then I want to talk to the referee."

When you immerse yourself in your work, your energies fully aligned with the task, creativity comes naturally. But getting to that immersion *is* the true challenge because there are plenty of obstacles that pop up on the way. Your life may feel like a video game with monsters and barriers aplenty. No matter how beautifully you've laid out your plans, there will always be something that will come along to knock everything awry. Be gentle with yourself when plans go askew. See it as a course correction. Keep in mind that nature abhors a straight line. Think of your work as taking the scenic route, with many twists and turns and wonderful surprises before you reach your goal.

It is common to go through our days as if we're on automatic pilot. The patterns we have constructed over the years tend to govern how we experience what is happening to us. But it is important to remember that there's no reason that the mental and emotional programming of the past has to create our perception of the present.

There is a world of difference between reacting to an event in your life and responding to it. When you re-act, you are acting again, repeating a previous action. To respond implies a spontaneous and appropriate response to the situation. The more you can see and feel each situation as a new one—even situations that appear to be the same old merry-go-round that you've been on before—remind yourself that *you are new*. Each day you grow and are changed by events. Each day it *is* a new you that is responding.

Over the years, we have learned that it's all right to feel good when something bad happens. It's all right not to take it personally when things go wrong. In fact, there may be nothing to do but laugh. There are significant losses that you need to grieve and mourn, but we're not referring to those here. We're talking about the daily hits where you are tempted to blame someone or something else. It might, in fact, be someone else's fault, but that is not important. What's important is how you work with the situation. You can feel powerless and be the victim, or you can probe deeper and discover how you could have avoided the problem. Almost invariably there is some piece, however small, that belongs to you in creating the situation.

If it is something that keeps coming up again and again with one particular person, you may want to approach him or her and ask sincerely how you can be of help. When someone is constantly dropping the ball, often it is because he or she needs more positive contact, not negative feedback.

The person may not even want to be in the job. If that is the case, it is far better to have this out in the open and work with it rather than to have an unconscious saboteur as a coworker. No matter what the reasons, there will always be things that go wrong—but how you respond to them is what's important. You can choose to get upset and overreact, or you can make alternative arrangements—which you'll have to do anyway, no matter how terrible—or terrific—you have made yourself and others feel in the process.

There remain, however, energy and disappointment around the mishaps, and these need to be discharged. Why not release these with humor? We have a standing joke with a friend with whom we commiserate over all sorts of snafus in our lives. She's single, and she teases us, "Well, at least you have someone to blame. You have each other." This always cracks us up because it reminds us of the great temptation to do just that, which we succumb to on more occasions than we'd like to admit.

Swami Beyondananda reminds us, "Humor has the power to expand our minds because it offers us a way to tolerate paradox." Also, laughter has the added benefit of energizing us.

SIX

The Native Genius of Intention

Flow with whatever may happen and let your mind be free. Stay centered by accepting whatever you are doing. This is the ultimate.
—Chuang Tzu

How can you think and hit at the same time?
—Yogi Berra

I propose that being on the spiritual path is such a natural and powerful urge that everyone's life, regardless of culture, obeys it. A path is just a way to open yourself to spirit, to God, to love.
—Deepak Chopra

Intention means what you intend to do, be, and have in life from your highest vision. The spiritual purpose is the divine motive that brings energy into form. What is your intention?
—John Randolph Price

Intention is a force that has the power to manifest what you want to happen. This occurs through consciousness by focusing on a specific overarching purpose. We find this in nature through the philosophy of teleology. *Teleology* is a Greek word that refers to the study of ends, goals, or purposes. It states that all biological organisms are directed to an end or shaped by a purpose. So in this view, plants grow roots with the aim of absorbing water and minerals from the earth. The tortoise has a hard shell out of its determination to ward off predators; the toucan has a large beak in order to crack hard nuts otherwise not edible; and the polar bear has a white fur coat so that it is camouflaged from its prey. The theological aspect of teleology relates to the doctrine of design and purpose in the material world.

Intent is a naturally driven process that facilitates evolution and has intrinsic organizing power. This is accomplished without conscious control and without effort. We understand the nature of intent because we recognize that Spirit created the universe through intent: God said, "Let there be light," and so it was. Spirit is the power behind intent. Consciousness is the agent.

The force of intention is always available to us, but we need to understand how to unlock its strength. It functions in the field of uncertainty, where there are no guarantees. You have to detach from the outcome of your action, which means even though there is an objective to reach and you have the resolve to arrive at that place, the truth is you are walking this path simply because you want to walk this path. The process is more important than the destination.

There is a letting go of expectation or attaining results even though the intention remains and the focus of energy stays on the present. You give up control and are willing to function in the field of uncertainty; your concentration is on whatever you are doing in the moment. Indeed, this principle is really the key to living life, because you are brought totally into the present without worrying about the future or regretting the past.

An intent begins with a general desire for something to happen. Focus and clarity arise from an insight, dream, idea, or vision of wanting something to happen. Energy, time, patience, and commitment are required to manifest it in the world. We have learned to appreciate the wisdom of the saying "Be careful what you wish for, because you're going to get it." Over and over again we have directly experienced the truth of this. As we held the vision and kept to our purpose, events would unfold to support the dream. They were unanticipated and unplanned, yet they were integral to the fulfillment of the intention.

Because intention is connected to the spiritual, it correlates with a willingness to trust in a generous universe, one that is friendly and supportive. If you don't possess faith in a well-disposed universe, then intention becomes problematic. Not only does intention require conviction, it also demands self-reliance.

Years ago when we decided to lease that five-story building in San Francisco to house both our workplace and living quarters, it was a major decision and a large financial commitment. At the time we wrote the deposit check and signed the lease agreement, it required all the money we had in the bank, several thousand dollars. We literally did not know where the next month's lease payment would come from. The decision was based solely on our intention and trust that the money would be there when the time arrived, as long as we kept doing what we needed to do. As time unfolded we were able to meet the next month's lease payment and continued to do so through the eight years we were there.

There is no magical list of do's and don'ts, which is what the rational mind hungers for. Intention is connected to the soul's purpose, so ultimately its origins are mysterious: "Take therefore no thought for the morrow; for the morrow shall take thought for the things of itself." You must set yourself on the path and deal with the twists and turns and crossroads when you come to them. Indeed, if you have determination, then the how-to's follow, not the reverse.

Single Focus

You may be involved in many activities, and your work may be multilayered, but to be effective it is crucial to focus your attention. Be discriminating, make a commitment, and center yourself in the present moment so that you are not distracted. Begin with a positive attitude, and realize that there is enough time available to get the work done.

Your mind needs to be clear to maintain a single focus. Our coworker Tom Greenaway exemplifies this attitude. We once asked him about this. He told us that he was inspired by an experience he had many years ago at the Miami airport. Because of bad weather, an airline strike, and many last-minute flight changes, a great number of people were standing in line at the ticket counter, all needing attention. He was among them.

He said, "I noticed that the woman at the counter was pleasant and patient with each customer. She greeted each one as if that person were her only customer, even though there were many disgruntled travelers in line. When I reached her I asked, 'How do you manage to maintain such composure and calm in the midst of this storm of people?' She said something that I've taken to heart ever since. 'I take each customer one at a time. I don't get ahead of myself and worry about how long the line is. I work with whomever is with me in that moment. The line will take care of itself.'"

Clarity of Vision

What you see is what you get. The worldview you hold determines what happens in your life. Your ideas, beliefs, values, rules, biases, experience, and attitude all coalesce to form your view of how the world works. As the Buddha said, "We are what we think. All that we are arises with our thoughts. With our thoughts we make the world." So it is all-important to clarify your vision. Sometimes we think we are clear about what we want but discover later that we were being guided more by our emotions and desires than by what is appropriate or necessary under the circumstances.

Some years ago, we purchased an old mineral springs resort with three other couples, and we held a vision of what would happen there. The vision did manifest, but much of what transpired had simply not been addressed in the original vision, so things turned out quite different from the way we had imagined.

As a group we had endeavored for years to deepen our self-understanding, our relationship to the planet, and our responsibility for improving life upon it. Our trust and respect for one another was very high. Several of us had spoken of our desire to leave the city, and it wasn't long before we could see the logic of pooling our resources and buying some property together in a rural setting.

Our dream was to find beautiful and affordable property that could house the different families separately and comfortably. Much to our collective amazement, this was successfully accomplished. However, we had not considered how we would live together on a daily basis, how each person would work within the group in the new setting, how we would compensate for the differences in the dwellings, or how we would cope with the changes that might arise, such as growing families and new babies. There was no room for unplanned events.

It was quite a shock to realize the assumptions each of us had made. We had begun with a vision, but it was only a partial one. On reflection, we could see that we had not gone far enough in clarifying it and fully addressing all of its ramifications. The late Swami Sivananda Radha, revered as one of the most important female spiritual teachers of the twentieth century, told us, when we explained that we had been following our heart, "Yes, it's important to follow your heart, but *it's also important to think clearly.*"

Mastering Monkey Mind

Our minds have been conditioned to think in certain ways, and our behavior has been molded into a specific shape.

Automobiles, airplanes, telephones, computers, electricity, and other technological advances have thoroughly altered our ways of living and the manner in which we perceive the world around us. Stress and tension are normal in this world. There is never enough time to get things done. We even have fast food for fast living. In *Resurgence of the Real: Body, Nature, and Place in a Hypermodern World*, Charlene Spretnak says we are living in the hypermodern era. The mind races to keep up, struggling in the midst of what appears to be mass chaos, confusion, and misplaced priorities.

Unless we can learn to relax our mind we are necessarily its servants, and thereby under its control. Sogyal Rinpoche says, "The ordinary ego-mind, with its disturbances and bothersome thoughts, is like a box of worms, all wriggling within fixed boundaries." He calls this state "monkey mind" and goes on to say, "The brain works best when we're *not* thinking"—a provocative idea for our Western minds, so used to *thinking* our way through life. For any of us who have spent nearly two decades being educated in school to think, this can be a challenging concept.

According to Sogyal, "Transforming one's attitude is the first principle. Observe and see your state of mind...remove the aggression, slow the speed. Aggression and speed are the two dangers of the time." He advises us to "allow thoughts to arise and settle...after that comes clarity. It's not the thoughts that matter, it's the *thinking* of the thoughts."

High stress, tension, and worry are products of our capacity to generate so much mental chatter. Buddhism has a larger definition of mind than we in the West have come to accept. The good news is that the delusions and worries plaguing us are not permanent. *There is hope,* and the solution is within our own power. If we are willing to slow down, sit quietly, remove the aggression, and be kind to ourselves, then we can begin to dispel the obstacles.

Sogyal says, "Give yourself a break. The nature of mind is such that mind will find its blissful state; everything is in the mind; enlightenment is there; wisdom coexists with confusion. Mind is the root of it all. Get to the heart of it. Perfect the goodness in order to tame, to understand.... Meditation is removing the unnecessary mess, clarifying our natural self. Just as water clarifies when you allow it to settle, the same is true with the mind."

So the choice is yours. By slowing your rapid pace and making it a priority to let go of the "thinking mind" by creating a time for meditation whenever and wherever appropriate, you can begin on the path to calmness and clarity, always remembering that the Buddha is not *out there.* The Buddha is within, and you have only to clear away the clouds to experience the open sky of an enlightened awareness. According to Buddhist philosophy, clarity is the innate nature of your mind, and it is thought that obscures it.

It is within your power to let go of your attachment to thoughts. Instead of dwelling on a thought, you can release it. Worries become solid when you make them concrete by dwelling on them. Sogyal advises us to see our thoughts as waves, rising up and then dissolving back into the great ocean. All of us have habitual patterns within our minds, so this process of letting go of thoughts is both difficult and simple. When we have trouble releasing a thought, it is useful to use the meditative technique of returning to the breath. By focusing on the breath, breathing in, breathing out, the thought is naturally released and we can begin again. You can do this anytime, anyplace: in the office, car, meeting room, or washroom, while changing the baby or buying groceries. If it were a pill, this exercise would be listed as the most effective cure for hypertension that science has ever discovered.

Simple Acts as Catalysts

Whatever you are doing, no matter how seemingly insignificant or meaningless, it's important that you do it with attention and awareness. Buddhists use the term *mindfulness* to describe the state in which one is aware that one is aware. It is this quality that you want to bring to the work you do, so that the consciousness of self is absorbed by the activity of the work itself. It's not something that is accomplished once and forever. It is more like doing the dishes — it needs taking care of after every meal.

You can teach yourself the good habits of paying attention. Begin with small things, such as noticing your environment. Do you turn the light off when leaving the room? Be present with other people — can you remember what color your friend was wearing today? Did you make eye contact with him or her? When you walked to the car from the store, did you hear the birds singing? Did you notice the leaves changing on the trees shading the parking lot? As you develop the ability to be attentive and aware, you will find life and work more engaging and meaningful because it actually becomes a spiritual practice. When you bring this focus to your work, your expression of commitment is visible, and it also inspires others.

Our former coworker Nita, mentioned in the previous chapter, recently told us of learning the value and meaning of the phrase "pay attention." She says, "The meaning of 'pay attention' is not just the words 'pay attention.' It is stop, listen, and look at your environment, each and every small detail. Every tiny thing counts because those little things add up to something big. Don't just gloss over details, look at them carefully. Take them apart, process them through your mind, and don't tell yourself there isn't enough time. I simply nailed each detail of every little thing, pulling it apart and putting it back together in a cohesive manner. Stop and do it. I'm doing that with every part of my life now and it is really paying off."

We've all seen living exemplars of this integrated approach to work. Most often they are found in the ordinary workplace. For instance, we know someone who is principally a carpenter but actually possesses many talents that he interweaves with his carpentry. He is a designer, architect, economist, planner, artist, craftsman, and more. It is wonderful to watch him work because of his singular commitment to applying his talents and skill to getting the job done, whatever it takes. The care he gives his work is his hallmark.

We find ourselves attracted to the energy and integrity of this man, because his approach to work inspires and energizes us. What you see is what you get. There is no split between who he is as a person and his outer expression through work.

Perseverance and Building Momentum

Once you begin to work on the plan to reach the goals you've set, don't stop. Each of us has a deep reservoir of energy. To this you need to add your commitment, your willingness to hang in there, no matter what. Others will notice and be drawn to your energy and your passion. Perseverance is essential and will enable you to effectively meet the challenges and move through them. You need to build momentum, and it's difficult to do so if you're continually stopping and starting. We ascend the mountain, reach the summit, then come down and cross the valley until we get to the next mountain.

After reaching the summit, returning to the valley seems a less heady experience. Spiritually, however, it is no different. It is just another experience. We're the ones who choose how to perceive the experiences of the summit and the valley. So if we're experiencing the valley as "less than," it becomes easier to stop altogether. Allow the experience of the valley to unfold. You may be pleasantly surprised by what can take place there.

When you continue to persevere in the middle of the valley, it keeps the momentum going; and you never know who's watching. The most surprising developments can occur when you least expect them. We now look on what we call "miracles" as natural occurrences. Often these happen during or immediately following a time of great testing of our commitment. This is yet another reason to keep your focus clear and not get distracted, even if it seems like a fallow period.

A woman in a workshop once told us how she started a business to encourage women to follow their dreams. At first every effort she put forth brought positive results. After about nine months, however, the energy stopped, and nothing the woman did seemed to get it started again.

She began to doubt her own vision, feeling that perhaps this was not her heart's calling. We advised her to persevere. It is not always going to be smooth sailing, and just because your dream project gets off to a good start doesn't mean there won't be some rough water ahead. Just after that workshop, she met another woman who shared and complemented her dream. Now they are working in partnership; and in just a few months the energy has begun to flow once more.

Someone once wrote to us about our programming and used the phrase "relentless in its possibilities" to describe our endeavors to continue producing and broadcasting positive, inspiring, and empowering ideas over the airwaves. During the first seven years of our work, we produced a four-hour live program every Saturday night. To make this happen required giving up our weekends. There were twelve of us who would come together on Saturdays to meet for most of the day and plan the evening's broadcast as well as future programs. These long sessions would be followed by the live broadcast from 8 P.M. to midnight. We would usually retire to a local restaurant afterward, and eventually get home early Sunday morning and spend the whole of that day sleeping and recovering. And we loved it!

The dedication of everyone involved helped to establish the standards and values that permeate our work to this day. As the *I Ching* often advises, "Perseverance furthers."

Aligned Action

The extent to which you can be one with your work is the extent to which you will do it with excellence. In sports this is called "being in the zone." When you're able to work in a fully integrated way, with your actions, words, thoughts, and feelings in alignment, and following your intention, then your work is obviously compelling.

In practice, though, many mundane details will come up that are not compelling, no matter how excellent your attitude toward your work. In Zen monasteries the monks perform manual labor of all types, and this *samu,* or "work/practice," is part of their training. The aim is for the mind to become so focused that self-awareness dissolves and the work becomes valued for its own sake, not for its result or what it may lead to. To the Zen practitioner, every act, no matter how menial, becomes a living expression of Buddha-mind, and therefore no work is beneath one's dignity.

When you approach work in this way, the small self or ego awareness is submerged, and you become one with the activity. This is where work is like meditation, and you are completely unified.

J. Krishnamurti said, "Meditation is not separate from daily life. If it is separate it merely becomes an escape, a romantic imagination. Real meditation is to be concerned with one's behavior, one's relationship — not only with one's own little family, but with the world." Work at this level creates a charismatic energy that attracts and inspires. We find meaning in our work rather than having to search for it somewhere else. According to Joseph Campbell, "We're so engaged in doing things to achieve purposes of outer value, we forget that the inner value, the rapture that is associated with being alive, is what it is all about."

Personal Responsibility

Moving forward with intention includes taking full responsibility for all aspects of the work we are doing. This applies to both positive and negative qualities, experiences, relationships, and whatever takes place in life, even though we are tempted to say, "It's not my fault; it's out of my control; I'm a victim of someone else's decision or action."

Taking full responsibility is the way to start to separate what is yours and what is another's. This doesn't mean that you accept responsibility out loud for everything going on around you, but that you make a practice of asking yourself certain questions before you start blaming others. Asking "How have I created it this way?" produces inner reflection and can help clarify what might otherwise be a blurred picture of why things are the way they are.

A few years ago, Diane Kennedy Pike and Arleen Lorrance taught us a technique of looking at a given situation or set of circumstances as a waking dream, analyzing it for understanding just as we would examine a sleeping dream. This is another way of getting beneath the surface appearances and discovering the roots of what is taking place. Many onerous issues that arise during work situations, such as financial pressures, interpersonal problems, lack of energy, boredom, and resistance to authority, can be effectively addressed this way.

Magic Is Alive

When you are clear about your intention and at peace with yourself, aligned and moving with purpose in your work, then magic happens. People appear, affinity projects emerge, support from unimaginable quarters suddenly manifests. What you need to accomplish your vision will become real, because of the natural attraction your clarity of purpose and focused energy create. Your own zest for life and work will naturally lead you into the here and now, where anything is possible and life is no longer defined by its usual limitations. You can feel the future unfolding as you relax into being in the moment, secure in the intention that what you are doing is the right action at the perfect time.

❖

SEVEN

Sacred Labor: The Soul of Work

Our age has its own
particular mission... the
creation of a civilization
founded upon the spiritual
nature of work.
—SIMONE WEIL

Fortunate is the person who
has worked hard and has
found life.
—THE GOSPEL OF THOMAS

You must be the change you
want to see in the world.
—MOHANDAS GANDHI

It isn't enough that we have
"meaningful" work. What is
also required is work that
satisfies the soul.
—THOMAS MOORE

What is really important is
not so much what work a
person does, but what he
perceives he is doing it for.
—WILLIS HARMAN

"You have the right to work, but for the work's sake only. You have no right to the fruits of work. Desire for the fruits of work must never be your motive in working.... Work done with anxiety about results is far inferior to work done without such anxiety, in the calm of self-surrender." It is thus, in the *Bhagavad Gita*, the Lord Krishna explains the principles behind the holiness of work to his eager student, Arjuna, who wants to know how to go about doing his duty. Here Krishna is extolling the importance of giving everything to your work without thought of reward or results, because this is the secret of work as spiritual practice. Clearly, there is a connection between the presence and energy we bring to our work and who we are. Joseph Campbell suggested that the decision about career "is to be a very deep and important one, and it has to do with something like a spiritual requirement and commitment."

Deep within each of us is an authentic self waiting to emerge. You may be tempted to copy others because they look cool or because other people admire them. We can learn something from the acorn—an acorn will always grow up to be an oak tree. A friend reminds us, "No matter how many redwood affirmations an acorn recites, it will still grow up to be an oak. Attending the very best redwood-tree schools in the world and studying with the very best redwoods, and eating the food that is most appropriate for redwoods, will not change its acornness. It would be far more appropriate for that acorn to discover its acornness, and commit to being the very best acorn it can be, so it will grow into the very best oak."

Enormous power and strength is available when you act from your essential nature. Philosopher and healer Patricia Sun tells us, "The most powerful thing you can do to make the leap into personal authenticity is to begin to consider, from this moment forward, that everyone you meet can read your mind."

Oh, what a scary thought! Think about it, though. Isn't this the only way to be true to your own life? Life transforms when you speak the truth. A phrase we have borrowed from our friend Angeles Arrien and often use is, "Tell the truth with kindness." When there is an absence of conflict between who you are and what you do, then your actions are positively contagious. Mother Teresa is an example of someone clearly aligned with her purpose. This tiny woman, acting from her inner truth, lives in such a way that others have flocked to help, ultimately waking millions of people to the power of compassionate, unselfish love.

Connecting with the Invisible World

By recognizing your inherent connections to the invisible or spiritual world, you will greatly enhance your creative intelligence. There is so much more to life than material reality. When you give credence to nonmaterial realities, you will have that much more support for the work you are doing. Regular attention to prayer, meditation, reflection, dreams, sacred rituals, offerings, solitude, and other activities are some of the ways to maintain your connection to the invisible world and honor its energies. The key is being willing to ask for help and surrendering to the mystery that is present. You may have one or several beings, spiritual teachers, ancestors, or saints you resonate with and call on periodically.

An excellent example of a society where many of the

people work in ways that blend the outer with the inner is in Bali, an island in the Indonesian archipelago. It was our experience in the countryside of Bali that work and play are fully integrated. The traditional Balinese people work just enough to take care of their essential material needs — food, shelter, and clothing. Frequently, their work is also their art or craft, because creativity and beauty are paramount.

It is not unusual to meet a Balinese who works as a maître d' in a restaurant or a clerk in a hotel and is also a fine artist, musician, woodcarver, or dancer. Others are able to combine their creativity with making money. Most of their creativity revolves around their religious practices and their community. They approach all of life as spiritual, and so their religious offerings and rituals occur in every aspect of daily life, including their work.

The Balinese are in touch with the invisible world. When we were in Bali we were curious about a Balinese woman we saw coming quietly into the courtyard of our hotel every morning. She carried a tray of folded palm leaves on which lay some rice, flower petals, and a bowl of water. The mysterious woman turned out to be the owner of the hotel, making a daily offering to the spirits of the place.

When we drove along the back roads, we noticed ancient shrines that seemed to have been long abandoned. However, upon closer inspection we saw an offering of freshly picked flowers laid at the base of each one. Every acre of Bali seems to be cared for in this way — individuals taking responsibility to honor the invisible energies of each place. We witnessed this in rice fields, in shops, at markets, in hotels, in homes — everywhere. In this way the Balinese maintain the connection with the spirits of the place. It inspired us to adopt a ritual of our own upon returning home. This can be done for your place of business as well. In Bali every shop and restaurant had evidence of an honoring ritual.

Nurturing Home and Place Ritual

Notice the cycle of the moon, and on the days when it is full and new, make an offering expressing your gratefulness for this life you share with other living beings. You will need the following items: a lettuce or cabbage leaf; a teaspoon of cooked rice, potato, or corn; a small bowl of water; a stick of incense; and a flower. Then place the food on the leaf. The leaf provides an organic plate for the food, which represents life-sustaining nourishment for our bodies. Add the flower to your arrangement. This represents beauty, which nourishes our spirit.

Take this offering outside along with the stick of incense, which represents the breath, and the small bowl of water, representing the most precious substance on the planet. Place the leaf at the base of a tree, plant, or bush in some corner of your yard. If you don't have a yard or an appropriate outside space, place the leaf by one of your house plants. Light the incense and place it next to the leaf. Holding in your heart a sense of gratefulness, dip the flower petals in the water and flick some water drops on the plant under which your offering rests, and pray that this plant will enjoy a long and healthy life. Thank it for its life. Let it know by your prayer that you are grateful that it has enriched your life with its beauty and its oxygen. If the plant is struggling, commit yourself to helping it by nurturing it in whatever way you can. Do this ritual twice a month, at the full moon and the new moon, which are auspicious days in nature's calendar.

Plan to go around your home or workplace over the course of a year so that you acknowledge all of your immediate surroundings. In this process you may find there are some places that especially call to you, that make you feel safe and happy. Note where these are; they are power places for you, and you can use them whenever you feel the need. This ritual helps you to build a compassionate resonance with the natural world and not only creates a healthier environment, but also increases your personal health—physical, emotional, and spiritual.

Maintain Your Inspiration

Keeping in touch with your inspiration is crucial. Even though you won't feel inspired all the time, it is good to raise your head occasionally and reconnect with why you are doing what you are doing. In our work area we have placed sacred images, meaningful photographs, powerful quotes on wall plaques, and other reminders that make our environment supportive. Human beings have a natural tendency to hunker down into tasks. We need little reminders to help us see the larger picture in the midst of our smaller undertakings. Some simple ways to do this are by taking a deep breath, going for a short walk, and having a vase of flowers nearby so that you become aware of their perfume from time to time.

Next to her workspace Justine has a sign with a quote

from the Welsh poet Gyen Thomas: "Don't expect life to make sense." Immediately under that there is another sign: "Take joy in the absurd." This helps her to lighten up when she's caught in the swamp of details and timelines.

We also have created several altars in our home and at work for the specific purpose of assisting us to keep in touch with the sacred. These are places where we have arranged things that remind us that we are not alone in this life, that help us to remember there are energies and people who both love and support us. One of our altars is quite ecumenical. It has feathers and semiprecious stones, gourd rattles, and a Tibetan *dorje* and bell. There are pictures of Sogyal Rinpoche, Swami Radha, and Thomas Merton. There is a statue of the Goddess of Willendorf and an image of Christ standing next to one of the Buddhas, a photo of the Dalai Lama, a bottle of rice collected from a ritual, and a small Easter basket. There is also an icon of Shiva and a photo of our grandchildren.

Over the years a strong field of positive energy has been created by the good intentions we have brought to our altar. We make sure to keep it dusted and clean. We pick up different objects from time to time, allowing the feel of them to reconnect us to what they symbolize for us. It is a dynamic place, reflecting the love and energy we give it. When arriving we often shake a gourd rattle, play a clay flute, or make up a song of appreciation for all it represents in our lives. When we first sit down at one of our altars we will purify it by fanning it with smoke from sage, cedar, or incense. We then call in our spirit helpers and guides. Keeping fresh flowers on the altar helps maintain an attitude of gratefulness for all the many blessings in our lives.

We maintain several well-constructed bird feeders outside our office window and keep them filled with unsprayed seed. The birds seem to appreciate our efforts. Our friends and coworkers say that our office should be listed in the *Bird and Breakfast Guide*—at least twenty different species of birds visit us regularly, and we see many more during migration season.

So often when we are in the middle of chaos, a family of acorn woodpeckers will perk us up by swooping down and making their laughing sounds. Immediately all work stops, our thinking is put on hold, and we just watch the birds being themselves. They refresh us, change our focus, and expand our view. Even as we write, a flock of more than thirty wild turkeys is milling about just outside the windows.

Sacred Is Real

During our first few days in Bali, Michael kept hearing about double ikat weaving and the aboriginal Bali Aga people, who claim an ancestry that predates the influx of the Javanese Hindus beginning in the tenth century. Literally, *Bali Aga* means "Balinese mountain people."

Only a few Bali Aga villages remain on the island, and Tenganan is one of the most famous. Inhabited by about 400 people in 125 families, it is the last true commune left in Bali and is a very wealthy village by local standards. It is the only place in Bali where *gringsing,* or double-ikat handweaving, is still practiced. *Ikat* is an Indonesian word meaning "bind" or "know." In straightforward ikat the warp (vertical threading on the loom) is stretched on a frame before weaving commences. The weft (horizontal) threads are bound according to a certain pattern and then dyed. The bound areas resist the dye, although some dye seeps under the binding, contributing to the characteristic blurred edge of ikat designs. These dyed weft threads are then woven into the plain warp threads.

In double-ikat weaving, both the warp and weft threads are dyed in this way and then woven so that the patterns coincide exactly. It takes several months to complete even one narrow scarf of double-ikat. The cloth has distinctive colors of reddish brown, off-white, and blue-black and is decorated with abstract patterns, floral designs, and sometimes images of the gods. The finished cloth is highly prized, held to have sacred and protective properties, and used in temple rituals in many villages.

The first impression of Tenganan is one of an English country village in medieval times. It is surrounded by a stone wall, with entrances at each of the four directions. After getting used to the nonwalled openness of Balinese houses, we were surprised to see that the houses of Tenganan had stone walls without windows. A single wide dirt street stretched upward in a series of tiers connected by cobblestone ramps. It was quiet, in contrast to most Balinese villages, which are resonant with sound. We walked past a doorway with a sign announcing a weaving exhibit. A clever inducement to trap the unwary tourist, we thought, and continued up the street. But someone called us back. As we passed through the darkened doorway, we entered a cornucopia of color, a living museum of objets d'art. There were sculptures, paintings, rich tapestries, woven baskets of varying sizes, and more—literally a treasure trove of Balinese art and craft. It took our breath away.

As our eyes adjusted to the dim light, we realized that

this was a family compound. Two young women were weaving cloth at separate looms, and there was an older woman as well. In the back, a man worked on a basket. As we expressed interest in some of the pieces, he came forward to help us. His command of English was impressive as he answered our questions.

There was an entire wall of double-ikat cloth hangings of varying sizes and lengths, which represented years of human labor. Even though these *gringsing* textiles are expensive by Balinese standards and highly prized by collectors, the cost still works out to about a dollar a day for the labor involved. Clearly, this labor is not performed just for the money. Indeed, this fact had puzzled us since we first heard about double-ikat. Why would people spend months, even years, of their lives making cloth like this?

As Michael stood staring at the lengths of cloth in front of him, Justine held an ikat cloth out to him, saying, "Isn't this beautiful?" As she did so, the man of the house, learned in the ways of Western shoppers (as are many Balinese), realized he had a live prospect on the line and began the process of reeling in the catch. However, as Michael listened to this villager describe the process of making the *gringsing,* he soon realized that what he was holding in his hands was a holy object, created out of love for Brahma, Vishnu, and Shiva (the Hindu trinity of Creator, Protector, and Destroyer). The weaving of each thread was a sacred act, and the final result was a complete prayer. He was filled with awe as he began to appreciate the intention and dedication behind this work. It has been said that "God lives in the details." Never has Michael seen stronger evidence for the veracity of that statement.

Trust in the Ordinary

Most of us have been trained to think of life as a series of special moments interspersed with the ordinary dailiness of existence. Stephan Rechtschaffen, M.D., the author of *Timeshifting*, says, "We live through the mundane events as though they are blips on the way to the big stuff." Our lives are filled with images that support our addiction to the next "high" moment. When was the last time you sat on a park bench, without any agenda, and observed life unfolding around you?

One day we were early for a dinner date with another couple. Our table was not yet ready, so we went across the street to a little town-square park. In that moment we realized, while watching some kids on skateboards, that we had been running from one intensity to another. Even our dinner date would involve intense conversation, which we love. And there we were, waiting for the intensity to begin again. It's an addiction. We must relearn the happiness of being ordinary.

Commitment

Commitment is a moment-to-moment process. You need to do it daily, hourly, continually. You make a choice in every action you take. Ask yourself, "Does this take me closer to my dream?"

Consider the covenant with your own vision as a precious friend. You must give your friend the gift of your attention. When you find your time being whittled away by serving someone else's dream, you place at risk the bond you are building with your own. If you commit to being a good gardener, you must put in time and practice gardening. There is no other way to do it.

If you find yourself faltering, check out your core beliefs. Ask yourself, "Does my vision seem so unattainable that there's no point in even attempting this?" or "What will my life look like when I create what I want?" Are you afraid you might be successful, and then your life will have to change? Be assured that your life *will* change as you follow your heart's joy.

One of the German philosopher Goethe's most famous couplets has to do with taking action to fulfill your heart's desire: "Whatever you can do, or dream you can, begin it. Boldness has genius, power and magic in it." Most people talk about their dream, wonder about it, think about it, or worry about it. But if they don't *do* anything about it, they will eventually lose the gift. Commitment is an essential element in practicing true work.

Creating the Context

With faxes, E-mail, the Internet, and desktop publishing, you are undoubtedly inundated with interesting and useful projects. Also, there are plenty of people who want to enlist support for saving the trees or starting a center for teens. There are hundreds of extraordinary projects, but they may not be yours. Do not feel you must take them on because they are good ideas. Stay with what is vital to you.

When the inspiration first came to us to create a vehicle that would be inclusive of changing human values and cultural shifts, we felt the need to confirm the validity of our vision. So we made contact with some experts to solicit their feedback and talk about our fledgling idea. The response was overwhelmingly favorable. Interestingly enough, several of these people became close personal friends and have since become important supporters of our work. This is what we have come to call "creating the context."

The word *context* derives from the Latin *contexere*, "to weave together." It has to do with coherence and creating something that is able to hold together over time. So it becomes paramount to understand the whole framework in which your work takes place. Do your homework early to avoid the obvious potholes in the road. Use the library, attend conferences in your chosen field, contact trade associations, utilize the Internet, refer to the Yellow Pages, spend time in bookstores, write letters, make telephone calls, and speak with people who are knowledgeable. Our own personal research and development has unearthed valuable information and has led us to individuals who have have helped immeasurably to guide our work.

Over the years we've had many people come to us to get feedback on their own ideas. For the most part ideas are simply that—perhaps good ideas, but ideas nevertheless. We have given our share of advice to many, but the majority of these projects never came to fruition. However, once in a great while someone will come along and some time later we find their project is flourishing. There is a world of difference between "It's a good idea" and "It's as good as done, whatever it takes." One idea has an intellectual enthusiasm only, and the other is aligned with the heart, mind, body, and spirit.

Information and Wisdom

Another ever-present aspect of resistance takes the form of distraction. We live in a world today that comes up with new and improved forms of distraction each year. Just when you believe you are immune from buying another "toy," you see an announcement for the "fastest ever" computer with a bazillion megs of RAM. Then for the next five months you are off into cyberland, figuring out how to get the computer up and running. Television, videos, computer games, movies— all manner of entertainments are calling to us to sample their wonders. Life resembles a carnival midway at times, with its many booths beckoning us to pause and try our luck.

One of the most significant changes that has occurred since the end of the Second World War has been the rise in the level of information to which we are exposed. It has been estimated that in Western society today we are exposed to more information in thirty days than people a century ago were exposed to in a lifetime. There's so much coming at us it's difficult not to be distracted by it, but most of this "stuff" is useless as far as helping us live our passion. Indeed, much of it is pessimistic, causing us to go into fear and become paralyzed.

There's an abundance of information, yet a shortage of wisdom. Information comprises data, facts, and opinion, and usually its importance is merely relative. Wisdom, on the other hand, touches us deeply because it is timeless in its relevance and significance. Sift out the wisdom and go for it. Ignore the lowest-common-denominator, sensation-grabbing media distractions, and put that saved energy into your heart's call. Our advice: Put yourself on a healthy media diet, where less is more. Give up reading the front page of the newspaper and watching the six o'clock news. You'll find out everything you need to know from your friends and associates.

Spiritual Mentors and Guides

During the early years of our work we were fortunate to encounter several people who became mentors. Each of them entered our lives as a direct result of the field of energy generated by the vision that was being expressed. First among these was the late Dr. Haridas Chaudhuri, the founder of the California Institute of Asian Studies in San Francisco (now the California Institute of Integral Studies), an accredited graduate school bringing together the philosophies of the world in a Western academic context. Dr. Chaudhuri was immediately supportive and became not only a friend but one of the founding directors of the New Dimensions Foundation.

Like us, Dr. Chaudhuri had followed his heart's calling. He understood the process, the wild turns in the road, and the hard work required. He was a rare individual, a visionary academic who combined both intellectual prowess and spiritual practice. He came to San Francisco from India in 1951 at the invitation of Dr. Frederick Spiegelberg, who at that time was the philosophy chair at Stanford University. Spiegelberg had written to Sri Aurobindo, one of the spiritual giants of India during the first half of the twentieth century and the major proponent of integral yoga and philosophy. He asked him to recommend someone well versed in both Western and integral philosophy, and Aurobindo recommended Dr. Chaudhuri, who at the time was teaching at Bengal University. He had never met Dr. Chaudhuri, but they had corresponded over many years.

Upon receiving Spiegelberg's letter, Dr. Chaudhuri saw it as his destiny, since his spiritual guru, Sri Aurobindo, was recommending him. So he gave up the security of a tenured professorship and came to the United States to follow his path into the unknown. Within a few years Haridas Chaudhuri had become the most prominent and respected teacher from India in America. Almost all of the Eastern spiritual teachers who came to the United States in the 1960s and 1970s made their first public addresses under the auspices of Dr. Chaudhuri's Cultural Integration Fellowship in San Francisco.

Dr. Chaudhuri left a great legacy in the form of writings, talks, and a graduate school for higher learning. He did this by being faithful to his own agenda. He never saw anyone before noon, using the mornings for meditation and writing. His normal workday continued until late at night. He was open and inclusive, accepting of all teachings as expressions of the divine. Gentle and intelligent, he was a rare combination of pragmatism and far-seeing vision.

We feel blessed and privileged to have known him, and to this day we carry him in our hearts and feel his energy present in our work. He continues to serve as a model for us. With humility and a grateful heart, he saw his work as service to all.

Mentors can be living or dead. Michael calls on the late Thomas Merton, the Trappist monk who was both a prolific writer and dedicated contemplative. Growing up Catholic, Michael was aware of Merton and his first book, *The Seven Storey Mountain*, but it wasn't until Michael was well into his forties that Merton came to him vividly in a dream. The dream was of a cement-block building with a porch. Inside was a simple room with a refectory table, upon which a stack of black binders rested. A figure appeared, and Michael recognized him as Thomas Merton, who said, "I am ready for you now." The image was so strong that he woke Justine to tell her of this dream.

Some days later he was in a small bookstore and suddenly spotted a book, *The Hidden Ground of Love* by Thomas Merton. This was the first in a series of four volumes. He took it home hungrily, and thus began his apprenticeship to Merton. Now Michael's bookshelf is filled with books by and about this special monk. Each day he gets up and selects something randomly from those volumes to speak to him.

What is so extraordinary about Merton for Michael is that he was a contemplative in an order of monks who were essentially living in silence. Yet through the discipline of the Trappist order he was able then — and now, through his writings — to make an enormous contribution to the spiritual lives of so many. To Michael, Merton represents the energy of the monk within, as well as that part of him capable of probing his inner depths through writing. Merton brings spirituality and creativity together in a way that touches Michael's soul. Since this is an integral aspect of the work Michael does, it is obvious why Merton is such a powerful helpmate to him. Whenever he wants inspiration, feels blocked, or wants to unwind from a difficult day, he calls on Merton, either through meditative practice or through reading his writings.

Justine frequently turns to her guide and protector, Tara, the first feminine deity of Mahayana Buddhism. Tara is seen as the Great Mother, the embodiment of all the Buddhas. Her attributes include unobstructed compassion and the ability to liberate one from the eight great fears: doubt, desire, envy, avarice, wrong views, hatred, delusion, and pride. She is perfect peace, and yet she is unconquerable and victorious. When she stamps her foot, all the universes shake. She grants supreme merit and is the source of wealth. In her green form she is depicted as having one foot poised, ready to stride out and free all beings from danger, fear, and misfortune. Justine says, "I definitely want Tara by my side. When I invoke her in my daily practice, I am reminded of all the help available in taming my fears and gaining wisdom, because she is the Perfection of Wisdom."

Dedicate Your Day

Shortly after we get up each morning, we make it a point to "dedicate the day." We pray that whatever we do this day will be for the benefit of all life everywhere. The practice is simple, and serves to remind us of why we're doing what we're doing as well as providing some silent reflection before moving into the activity of the day. We also call on our "invisible guides," which are numerous and represent various energy forms intended to help us engage with our life and work. These guides are our ancestors, the ones we are acquainted with and those we are not, as well as the energies of all the saints and great teachers who have meaning in our lives, such as Jesus, Ramakrishna, Vivekananda, Gandhi, Our Lady of Guadalupe, Tara, Buddha, and many others. We imagine their blessings pouring down upon us and through us into our work to be of help to all sentient beings within our sphere of influence.

This daily dedication doesn't require adopting any particular religious doctrine or belief system. It is a matter of acknowledging capacities that each of us has within. You can choose an invisible mentor based on your own life path. Select as many as you feel you need. Sri Ramakrishna, the nineteenth-century Indian saint, used to say that we could attract anyone who had ever been incarnated on Earth simply by speaking the sacred sound *om* before their name.

Performing a dedication each day gives you a sense of connection and partnership with a larger order of reality, an order not influenced by the flotsam and jetsam that can disturb the calm as you move through your day. If you see life as a precious gift—not one to be taken for granted—and practice gratitude for what you have, then life will open its mysteries and wonders to you. Having awe for the sheer magnificence of life goes a long way toward helping you engage all its changes and challenges.

Working with Others

This is a good time to mention the importance of working well with others, especially if your dream necessitates creating an organization or community with people on a small or large scale.

No matter what your work is, you need the cooperation of others. And this is as it should be, because we are basically social animals and are happier when we're able to share our enthusiasms with other people.

One of the best opportunities about work is that we get to invent games that allow us to play together. As children we pretend to use money. But "grown-up" work is not much different—we make it all up. So why not do something that is fun, makes us happy, and contributes to others in a positive way?

In our work, we have learned to appreciate the value of synergy, where one plus one equals three and one plus two can be the equivalent of five. Creativity expands and momentum builds when two or more are gathered in the name of living your passion and honoring your spiritual voice. When you combine forces with another, you multiply the effects of your efforts exponentially. The two of us realize every day that without the other we would not be able to do as much as we do.

As you near a deadline—usually a self-imposed one—the tension that builds becomes your challenge to practice equanimity in the workplace. You have a great opportunity to learn the skill of being kind to one another when the temptation is great to become overly focused on the goal. Enjoying the time you spend with your coworkers *must* outweigh the inevitable momentary flares of tensions.

The bottom line of any of our accomplishments is, has our compassion grown with our business? Has our wisdom expanded with our budget? Has our laughter increased with our staff?

It's not that it's "make nice" all the time, either. As we've said before, the creative process is messy, and working with others puts an added spin on it. It resembles a litter of puppies—sometimes they are all comfortable, sleeping, snuggling, and warm in the spot they've found for themselves. Then one wakes up and moves. She pushes against her neighbor, who then steps on the head of the next one—and soon you have a pile of squirming, squealing, yipping puppies. It feels like warm, sleeping puppies when your desk is clean, your messages answered. You feel on top of things, everything is under control. Then someone suddenly steps on your head by coming in with a whole new project.

In working with others you must figure out a way of holding the energy while fanning the creative flames. It is a much more elegant process when each member of the team is willing and committed at the deepest level to grow and expand in consciousness. We need to become more conscious of our own actions and take *responsibility* for them. The "blame game" gets us nowhere. The good news is that as you start to take more responsibility, you also begin to do only what you love to do.

Go for Goodness for Goodness's Sake

Think the best of everyone on your support team. People respond positively to positive feedback and acknowledgment. Don't waste time and energy in reaction and criticism toward someone making a blunder. Simply address the problem clearly and communicate appropriately why his or her actions did not serve the vision—and then move on.

Extreme criticism and emotional upset not only is self-negating, but holds us back and is debilitating for others. Honor the Buddha-nature or Christ-nature within everyone and speak to that part of each person when addressing an error in judgment or an oversight. This does not mean you ignore mistakes and problems; rather, you place them in the proper context. Usually, a person's good qualities far out-weigh their weak ones. Keep this in mind and the path will be easier.

Humility and Gratitude

Whenever we see the Dalai Lama, we are struck by his humility. "I am just a simple monk," he says. Clearly, he stands for much more than that in the eyes of millions of Buddhists and non-Buddhists alike. Yet his manner is unassuming and self-effacing. This is the mark of a true leader who has reached mastery. He is at one with himself, so he radiates strength and power with gentleness.

You may know people who keep their lives simple and aren't out to impress anyone. They are naturally themselves, and it's wonderful to be around them. They listen attentively to everyone, ask relevant questions, and are genuinely interested in the views of others. They want to be of help, but are not interfering. Having this attitude leads to acknowledging the good fortune of our circumstances, beginning with the fact that we are alive, breathing, and healthy.

David Steindl-Rast, a Benedictine monk, speaks of beginning each day with gratitude, expressing gratefulness for sight as soon as we open our eyes, and continuing the practice throughout the day with each of our moment-to-moment encounters. He says, "Most of our day is gift after gift, if we wake up to it." Recognizing that we are blessed to be here at all gives us humility in the face of what can only be described as the Great Mystery. When we move through our day with this awareness, we are empowered to act responsibly and compassionately, even in the midst of great challenge. Being grateful helps us keep a broad perspective in the face of both good and bad circumstances.

EIGHT

Money

and

Wealth

*Money will come when you
are doing the right thing.*
—MICHAEL PHILLIPS

*Do what you love,
the money will follow.*
—MARSHA SINETAR

*The most precious things in
life are not those one gets
for money.*
—ALBERT EINSTEIN

*The wise and moral man
Shines like a flower on
  a hilltop,
Making money like
  the bee,
Who does not hurt the
  flower.*
—PALI CANON (500 B.C.)

Money—just what is it, and why does it cause so many problems? We know it is a means of exchange that comes in many forms, one of them a piece of colored paper to which we ascribe an agreed-upon value. Money also has hidden qualities that each of us has given to it, either consciously or unconsciously.

For example, riches are often equated with security and power. Some people think that money brings prestige or makes them more attractive, even popular. Others associate it with success, intelligence, or being accepted. Because of the place money holds in our society, there are countless qualities we project upon it.

Justine had an experience that revealed to her the unexamined beliefs she held regarding currency. We were batting around design ideas for a journal cover and someone noticed the similarity between our picture of Jacob Needleman, the author of *Money and the Meaning of Life*, and the picture of George Washington on the U.S. one-dollar bill. We got the inspiration to superimpose the author's image on a picture of the dollar, since financial wealth was the primary topic of his interview.

Justine copied a dollar bill on our copy machine. As she was walking away from the machine a feeling of guilt suddenly swept over her, and with it she heard an internal voice saying, "This is sacrilegious; we are doing something morally wrong." In that moment, the door to a deep-seated belief was opened, and these words appeared like writing in the sky of her mind: "Justine, you have placed dollars on your personal altar, and imbued them with spiritual meaning."

She realized the extraordinary value she had ascribed to money—not just for what it can buy, but because of the religious aura she placed around it. Unconsciously, she had turned the dollar into an icon. The feeling of guilt in her body was strong, as if she were about to draw a mustache on a picture of Buddha, or the Virgin Mary. However, her sense of humor surfaced and she laughed as she told her colleagues of her insight. We all agreed that this could be the perfect occasion for all of us to dig deeper into our personal "stuff" about legal tender.

There was another unguarded moment when Justine was able to view afresh her relationship with paper currency. She and Michael were flying to central Canada from Vancouver, and during the trip the flight attendant came down the aisle selling beverages. She offered each passenger a drink, and in turn each one gave her a piece of rather pretty paper with soft pink colors on one side, green on the other, engraved with an elegant picture of Queen Elizabeth. It struck Justine as a very uneven trade. Even though the paper was attractive, it was still only paper, and the passenger was receiving a tall, cool glass of orange juice in exchange.

Justine realized that she had no emotional attachment to Canadian cash. She hadn't grown up with it and had no history of using it as a medium of exchange. She was not, in fact, tuned in to the cultural consensus of Canadians that gave these pieces of paper meaning and value. This was the first time she realized that she had an emotional attachment to *her* form of money.

The attraction to money is a compelling force in our society. We make it, spend it, save it, lose it, and bet it. It can be a vehicle to support our highest aspirations and ideals. It has an impact on our lives in a multitude of ways. On a global scale, currency and economic forces shape national agendas, create conflict and wars, and produce social unrest, injustice, and oppression. The exchange of dollars, marks, francs, yen, pounds, and pesos finds its way into every aspect of life on the planet, so it behooves us to understand more fully how it relates to the meaning of our lives and our work.

The nature of currency is mutating. Money has become a series of digits on fiber-optic lines, passed from one computer to another without ever seeing the light of day. The economy is a collective conceptual reality, and is only as good as the agreed-upon belief of the majority of the population as to its inherent value. Outside our belief in it, it has no value. However, we receive daily reports on the Dow as if it were a living, breathing entity.

During the spring of 1996, it became publicly known that a Japanese trader had covered up the loss of several hundred million dollars in the worldwide copper market over a ten-year period. Though these losses had been occurring for years without public knowledge, no one had gone hungry as a result of them, no one had lost their house, and lending and borrowing had moved along in a natural flow. Yet with the news of the losses, the copper market fell and thousands of lives were affected, even though in one sense the losses were simply transposed decimal points on a computer screen. This is an example of the shared illusion in which everyone agrees on what is reality.

The Soul of Money

One of our friends and colleagues, Lynne Twist, presents workshops entitled "The Soul of Money." She says, "[We can] use money as another avenue to express the soulful human beings that we are."

She uses the metaphor of water to describe the flow of cash and how it works: "When water is moving and flowing, it cleanses, purifies, and makes things green. It creates growth and is beautiful. When it slows down and begins to sludge and be still, it becomes stagnant and toxic. This is also true of money." If you're having a difficult time letting money flow through your life, Twist says, "it's like trying to see the world through a toxic fish tank, and you can't see clearly." She goes on to say, "Money carries energy with it wherever it goes.... So one of my missions this lifetime is to enable people to assign money to fulfill their highest commitments, and to send it off into the world with love, with voice, with commitment, with vision."

So often the intrinsic value of a job is in what we are paid to perform it. You may love your job, hate it, or be ambivalent about it. It doesn't make any difference. What you need to know is that your employment brings you wages. Your passion may be something else entirely. Once you break the emotional association between work and wages, a new realm of possibilities is opened up and you are able to give your best to *all* your work, including whatever you do for income. No longer are you expecting your paid position to fulfill your need for meaning as well. Now you can clearly determine how much the paid job is worth relative to your real purpose. You may choose to reduce your paid time or change jobs to pursue more of what gives meaning to your life.

When Michael left his corporate position after eight

years, he didn't know what he would do next—and it didn't matter. He dissociated himself from needing the earnings and benefits that were keeping him locked into the job. Once he did this, thereby severing the tie that was the "security" a job provided, then he had the freedom to choose. So long as he stayed in the job, there was no freedom to choose, because the work situation was limited. Once he was able to discard the limitations of that job, even though it was a "good" job, he was released, and open to new possibilities.

Many people have opted to reduce their lifestyles and have given up high-paying employment in order to live more fulfilling lives. Getting rich is one thing. Your joy and purpose are quite another. Joseph Campbell described an experience of this: "If you follow your bliss, you'll have your bliss, whether you have money or not. If you follow money, you may lose the money, and then you don't have even that." The need for security can become a life-long trap. It probably inhibits more people from living their passion than any other single factor. It is the great illusion, and it must be broken.

We know someone who lives well, though simply, on approximately three hundred dollars a month. He is happy, fulfilled, and travels the world widely. How does he do it? He created a niche for himself as a freelance travel writer. All of his trips are paid for by his clients, and in addition he receives a fee for whatever he writes. He flies first class and stays in the best hotels. When not traveling he lives in a very small cabin, for which he pays a nominal rent, on the northern coast of California amongst some of the most spectacular scenery in the world. The vista is free. He is his own boss and only "works" when he wants to.

The Value of Money

Since we live in a world that collectively believes money is valuable, we need to look at exactly what that value is. Vicki Robin and the late Joe Dominguez, of the New Road Map Foundation and coauthors of *Your Money or Your Life*, have rightly suggested that money is equivalent to life energy: "Are you making a living or making a dying?" They go on to point out, "Money is something we choose to trade our life energy for. Our life energy is more *real* in our actual experience than money. You could even say money equals our life energy."

From this perspective, we begin to see how the money we earn is directly related to the amount and quality of time we spend in getting it. If we perceive money in this way, we will become more conscious about our moneymaking as well as our spending choices. Too many career choices are determined by how much income the profession will generate, to the exclusion of other considerations such as quality of life.

Our financial life does not exist separately from the rest of our life. We must look critically at the way we earn a living, and look closely at the quality of our lives. Poet and farmer Wendell Berry says, "The usual version of economics involves deferred satisfaction: You will do something you don't like in order to later buy the opportunity to do something that you do like. This seems to me to be the wrong way to go about it.... There's a lot of hatred of life involved in this, a lot of hatred of the informal catch-as-catch-can nature of actual daily life, in which the best pleasures often aren't foreseen or planned, and the worst disasters aren't necessarily forestalled by anything that anybody can purchase."

We must scrutinize all our assumptions about how we earn our livelihood. There are a limited number of hours, days, weeks, months, and years left to you, and how you use your life energy during this period — beginning now — is your choice. If you are working, you are trading life energy for income. Only you can establish new priorities for what you do with your energy, especially as it relates to what you receive in exchange. Become aware of this trade, which takes place with every transaction you make. Dominguez goes on to say, "Are you getting value in this exchange?" When you buy something, figure out how much life energy it is costing you. The answer may be illuminating.

Money was created for the purpose of facilitating the exchange of goods and services, not as a commodity in and of itself. However, over the past several decades, it has come to be viewed as *the* most valuable commodity. Indeed, as you read these words, people are making money through trading dollars for francs, lire for pounds, or yen for rubles.

The fact is, however, that money has no value other than what we give it. It is colored ink applied to paper and then reproduced. Remember Justine's story about using Canadian currency? The medium of exchange that we use today in the United States is essentially given value only by the faith that we have in the country.

Earning a living in our society has taken on a life of its own, and rarely do we stop and reflect upon it. Making money has become an end in itself. Jacob Needleman says, "Money has become for our generation what sex was for the earlier generations — a force that is at the back of almost everything people do, which we're not yet able to face without hypocrisy." Ask anyone how much they make or how much they have saved, and you have entered an extremely secret and emotional realm.

Within our own family and work relationship, our finances have served as one of the more powerful catalysts for taking us into uncharted depths, surprising us with their capacity to reflect our own growing edges. Exploring money and what it means to us has deepened and enlarged our relationship.

If you are interested in work as spiritual practice, you have to address the role money plays in your life. What does it symbolize? There are those who feel that work is a burden and who pursue dollars in the belief that when they have enough they will have the leisure time to devote to their dreams. This is unfortunate. One of the most significant problems with money is relating to it as a cause instead of a result. What's crucial here is to realize that money follows intention and purpose, not the other way around. We have known several people who put enormous amounts of energy into a new business with the idea that the endeavor would eventually generate so much income that they wouldn't have to attend to it, but would be able to turn their energies toward making a contribution in the world. If only they had directed this energy to their passion, they would have reached it sooner!

Doing something in order to earn the money to do what you want to do can become an endless merry-go-round. The work of the heart must be ever-present within you, and you must act on your passion each and every day. Do not put it off as some future event.

The Rules of Money

To what use do you put your money? The second law of Michael Phillips, author of the popular classic *The Seven Laws of Money*, is "Money has its own rules." Keeping records, budget planning, saving, borrowing, and spending are all aspects of the rules of money, and all need attention if you want to work in partnership with it. You must not be afraid of money, nor can you take it for granted. You must make friends with it. When you spend it, ask yourself, "Do I really need this or do I merely want it?" You may decide that you don't really need it but want it anyway. That's okay. The point is to make a conscious decision. You can use money badly or you can use it well.

Are you addicted to money? How much is enough? Being too attached to or greedy for dollars can cause misery and unhappiness. Appreciate money for what it can give— nothing more, nothing less. This is where you can become clearer about your wants and needs.

We live in an economic system called capitalism, which is based not on satisfying wants or desires but on creating them. This is crazy but true. Think about it: Do we really need another sugar-coated cereal, line of automobiles, or new clothing fashion?

In our society, where we worship consumerism, the motto seems to be "I buy, therefore I am." This is very self-centered and produces an I'm-going-to-get-mine-no-matter-what approach. It disregards the effects of our actions on ourselves and others, and makes acquiring money the be-all and end-all.

The market economy is fueled by basic human desire.

We are born with desire; it is written into our genetic code. We desire to feel our oneness with creation or, as some would say, with God. Desire is something that constantly pushes us. Marketers use this innate human quality to sell us more goods and more services. Our appetites are unending. But no matter how many goods we buy, they won't satisfy us, because in reality we are seeking qualities and not things.

Of course, we have to take care of basic needs such as housing, nourishment, clothing, and health. But the quality we most desire is to be unified with ourselves, with others, and with nature. When we are in this flow, we are in an enlightened state. Our thoughts, feelings, actions, and speech are in one accord. This is our true state, one of interdependence and connection.

Since Michael left a nine-to-five job, his life has been guided by what moves him deeply. Once he made a commitment to serve, his vision gradually became clear. He hasn't had a "real" job in thirty years, but he has never been limited by not having money. He began the quest with his wits, intelligence, passion, and limited personal resources. He had a dream, and he followed it. Money has been simply an artifact along the way. We do not mean to imply that following this path is easy just because you're doing what you want to do. Rather, we want to make clear that your attitude and intention are such that the obstacles you encounter along the way become challenges that push your edge and draw the best out of you.

True Wealth

The late Sir Laurens van der Post, who lived with the Bushmen of Africa's Kalahari Desert regions and called them "the ancient ones, the first people," points out that they had no concept of being separate and isolated. Wherever the Bushmen went, they belonged and were known. They were known by the land itself, by the stars above them, and by all the life around them.

Most of us have a deep desire for this sense of belonging. It is our heritage and a gift from our ancestors, but in modern-day life we have confused the desire for at-one-ment with the desire for possessions. Once again we have confused being with having. We think that through acquiring more we can actually *be* more, when in fact having less is likely to be more fulfilling. And the market economy is strengthened by this confusion. We keep buying in order to fulfill our desire, but stuff and things will never fill this longing. It can be satisfied only by the spiritual experience of knowing that we are one with the universe, with God's creation, with the great mystery.

The Buddha suggested making your home under a tree. It was his way of saying that the fewer encumbrances you have, the easier it is to find self-sufficiency and real freedom. All the great spiritual traditions have viewed material riches with a jaundiced eye because of the inherent dangers associated with acquiring them. The desire for things as ends in themselves becomes a trap that can prevent you from having true wealth.

Wealth is the perception we hold about life. Enjoy your wealth by examining what you already have in your life. Good health, friendship, love, caring, sufficiency, happiness, family, opportunity, creativity, and fulfillment are more accurate measures of true wealth than the sum of your possessions and bank accounts.

Each morning the sun rises on the horizon and begins to light the sky, no matter where you may live. Its rays bring warmth and energy to all living things. Appreciating the beauty and magnificence of nature is wealth. Being in love with your husband or your wife is wealth. Being blessed with a child is wealth. Having the caring and support of friends is wealth. You can't buy these. The wealth of the human experience is beyond money. It is the realization that we are connected to every other living thing in the world. Then the whole world becomes yours. This is what true wealth is all about.

It's not that there's anything wrong with owning things and having large bank accounts; it's how you behave in relation to your possessions and money. True wealth is having enough for your needs and being satisfied with that. It comes from a deep awareness of your spirituality and connection to your soul's purpose. When your work and life are based on what is inside rather than outside, then whatever you have is sufficient. This is true wealth.

NINE

The Circle of Work: Friends of the Heart

Somewhere there are people to whom we can speak with passion without having the words catch in our throats... a circle of healing. A circle of friends. Someplace where we can be free.
—STARHAWK

Everything the power of the world does is done in a circle.... The life of a [person] is a circle from childhood to childhood, and so it is in everything where power moves.
—BLACK ELK

Everything that lives, lives not alone, nor for itself.
—WILLIAM BLAKE

From a point comes a line, then a circle. When the circuit of this cycle is complete, then the last is joined to the first.
—SHABISTARÎ
(FOURTEENTH-CENTURY PERSIAN POET)

Through new technologies, advances in communication, and global travel, there is a greater awareness of the complexity of the issues facing humankind at this time. We are relearning how to engage with one another in work situations as well as social ones. There is a longing for the graciousness of past decades, but not at the price of ignoring the shadow side of human actions. We are living in the changing of an age, where homogeneity is not the dominant force. There is no outward, seemingly uniform structure to which all can claim allegiance. As choices become more and more complex, culturally agreed-upon values are not so clear. No longer do we live and work in a place where everyone agrees and sees life through the same lens, making it easier to move together in one accord.

This complexity affects our lives and work every day. In order for us to be happy in our work relationships, it is most important to remember that we are all connected. There is no act, no matter how small or seemingly trivial, that does not add to and consequently influence the whole. In *A Far-off Place*, Laurens van der Post wrote, "Nothing that is ever done is ever wasted or without effect on life. Nothing is ever so insignificant as to be unimportant. Everything in life matters and ultimately has a place, an impact, and a meaning."

Danah Zohar, author of *The Quantum Society*, reminds us of the practical reality: "We can no longer function as interlocking bits of isolated matter, as it were. We need a whole new model of ourselves which can account, in a positive way, for how it is that we impinge on each other, how it is that we really are, literally, deeply, an interwoven community."

Not only are human beings interconnected, but everything in the universe is interconnected. Every element is related, and each of us is part of the larger community and web of life. Futurist and author Barbara Marx Hubbard has said, "The very force of survival which may have made us separate from each other and competitive in the past is drawing us toward feeling connected, cooperative, co-creative." Barbara feels there is a "universal human" implicit in the human race and inside each of us, which is, "by the very force of the evolutionary crisis, being called forth."

We each make a difference, and it is essential to become aware of that fact. Because we are all connected, we need to learn to listen deeply to one another as well as speak from our hearts. It is this deep listening and speaking that builds a foundation of trust and affection within any community. Our work environment is as surely a community as a church, temple, mosque, or ashram environment.

It is critical to the health of our communities, work and otherwise, to strive together for the good of *all*. This includes grappling with one another with honesty and integrity. It is our natural state to be in community, to support one another and receive support. The Reverend Mary Manin Morrissey points out, "It's really important to have partners in our believing—people who help hold our dream as sacred in their mind and heart, who encourage us."

Often it is the technology of the age that reflects the unfolding of a new consciousness. The Internet and the World Wide Web are outer expressions of what's taking place inside each of us—the recognition of our singular place *and* connection within the whole. The paradox is that we live in a time of great alienation from one another as well.

The 1970s have been characterized as the "Me Decade." Upon closer inspection, however, we can see a remarkable tide of energetic young people coming out of the turbulent sixties, turning inward to look deeply at their core beliefs and values. It was a decade in which women began to raise their voices, and the women's movement renewed itself with great vigor. Many who grew up in the Christian tradition expanded and deepened their experience of spirituality. Seekers began to explore and become practitioners of a variety of wisdom traditions such as Buddhism, Hinduism, Islam, and many other spiritual paths. They went into self-help programs such as est and Lifespring, and twelve-step programs expanded exponentially. And citizens quietly returned to their communities with a commitment to make a difference for the better in their neighborhoods, in their workplace, in their families, and in the world.

The true "Me Decade" came in the 1980s, which was marked by such self-aggrandizing activities as hostile takeovers of companies with junk bonds and the frenzied feedings on savings and loan institutions, the result of which has saddled the American public with an enormous debt for decades to come.

Despite all of this, as we move toward and into the next millennium, the idealism of the 1960s is alive and well, and ever more grounded in practical everyday activities. At the grassroots level there are significant changes in the culture, not only in America but worldwide. Socially and spiritually relevant communities and organizations are on the rise, and these serve as a context in which positive engagement with others can take place.

Building Community

People's hunger for community is growing in this time of great change. Meeting with others in mutual support is one of the most fruitful activities we can do. Even though our lives have become more and more complex and our calendars crowded with activities, it is truly important to make time to meet regularly with a support group.

Sedonia Cahill and Joshua Halpern, coauthors of *Ceremonial Circle*, speak eloquently about joining in circle: "The ceremonial circle is the most effective form for breathing new life into the soul and spirit of human interchange, for inspiring renewed personal vision and for recreating a cohesive community. The circle allows the individual to feel part of a large being that has a life of its own and whose power is solely available to nurture. The connection between people in a ceremonial circle creates the threads that will weave the human species back into the Sacred Hoop of Life."

We have been participating in circles for many years. The circle is a place where we begin to rediscover our natural way of being with ourselves and others. This has enabled our work to remain fresh and vital. If someone were to ask us what is the single most important activity for personal growth that we've discovered, we'd answer that it is sitting in sacred circle with others. In doing this we have stretched and deepened far beyond what we could have accomplished alone. We have gained empathy and compassion not only for others but for ourselves, and we have collectively connected with the Great Mystery. When we've been in conflict and turmoil, bringing our pain to the circle has been an act of healing. The diversity of the circle expands our horizons and feeds us deeply; we return to our own work refreshed and reinvigo-rated, having gained new perspectives. Our landscape is broadened, and our sense of love and connection expanded.

Creating Your Own Circle

Participating in a company of people committed to deep lis-tening and speaking from the heart brings a wholeness into our lives. In our circles, we practice other ways of being beyond our habitual selves and we share our stories with one another at leisure. Television journalist Bill Moyers says, "Stories are the way we organize our response to the world.... Listening to others, and having them listen to you, is a way to grow your own faith."

Circles can be as varied as flowers in a garden. Some are gender-specific, such as men's circles, women's circles, or spe-cific to sexual orientation, such as gay people's circles. Some are mixed. You can choose to gather with people of your own age and stage in the life cycle, or you can choose to meet with people of all ages. You can meet around certain topics or for special celebrations and/or rituals. A circle can be a study group or a group that makes music. It can meet once a week or once a month. We have several circles that meet only twice a year, but for at least three to four days at a time. This allows for a very deep process to unfold.

It is often hard at first to make the time to attend the circle because the rhythms of our lives race along at a mad pace. But after you have been meeting together for some time and have reaped the benefits of gathering in such a way, the scheduling becomes much easier because it will organi-cally become a priority.

Circles have no leader, but you may decide that one person will guide or set the tone for a specific meeting. The next meeting may be guided by someone else, thus passing the responsibility from person to person. Everyone literally sits in a circle, so that each person can see everyone else. It is better to keep the group rather small, say a dozen people, so that everyone can speak and feel they have been heard. But this is not a rigid rule. Some circles do quite well with twenty or thirty people. The wisdom of the group will move naturally from person to person. Sometimes you'll find yourself making the most profound utterances, and at other times it seems that nothing sensible or coherent will come out of your mouth.

In one of our groups, someone told of a dream that seemed to embody the magic of meeting in this way. The dream was of a desert in which a number of people stood, each wrapped and asleep as if in a cocoon. Alongside them were two or three whose wrappings had peeled away like banana skins, and their eyes were open. As the dream moved on, these unwrapped persons became encased in cocoons while others peeled theirs off. So, at any one time, two or three were able to see clearly while the rest were asleep, each spending some time in each state.

This was a dream about the strength of sitting together. Different people will be awake at different times. It is not incumbent on any one person to always lead or be watchful. We unzip ourselves from our cocoons at different times, and are able to hold the light for others by truthfully telling our own story.

When we visited Ireland, Michael was inspired by the many ancient circles of stones we found there. He asked, "What was the motivation that prompted these people to transport these huge stones over great distances?" In many cases the stones have been relocated from hundreds of miles away. The insight that he had was that these people from long ago wanted to communicate to the generations that followed what was most important to them. They wanted the message to endure, and so it has. He says, "The wisdom they are communicating to us is the importance and value of coming together in circle." The circle is the place where stories are the coin of the realm and the listener grows rich.

We are reminded of the writing of Barry Lopez in *Crow and Weasel*. In this book, Badger says, "I would ask you to remember only this one thing. The stories people tell have a way of taking care of them. If stories come to you, care for them. And learn to give them away where they are needed. Sometimes a person needs a story more than food to stay alive. This is why we put these stories in each other's memory. This is how people care for themselves."

A Sacred Container

Gathering together in circle, we practice letting go of our agendas, our opinions, and our judgments. Here we learn to suspend our reactions, even those inside us, and go deeply into the unknown to find our true voice. Here we practice being supported by others and supporting others in their fullness of being.

A good circle becomes a sacred container made by its members. It is not so much a physical haven as it is an energetic container. Over the years we've found a few basic principles that help to make a circle gathering dynamic, nurturing, cohesive, and exciting.

One of the first and foremost requirements is for people to show up when they say they will and for the fellowship to end at the time agreed upon. It means putting the meeting in your calendar as an important event and giving it priority, investing in its creation with energy and intention.

Another ingredient that provides integrity is to begin by inviting in the sacred in whatever way seems appropriate. This can be as simple as lighting a candle and saying a prayer, or it may be a more elaborate ritual. The beginning of the gathering needs to be something that helps to set the space apart, separate from the rest of your life. The opening might be shared by different members at each meeting. June Singer puts it this way: "If we recognize that we're trying to connect to something mysterious and unknowable, and that all these different forms are the ways that different people use to come to the same place, then we can respect each other's rituals and realize that we're all embarked on something that is a human reality."

Drumming is an effective way to begin a circle. In a short time this powerful activity brings body, mind, and spirit into harmony with others. The particular drumming described in the following section is simple yet profound.

Harmonizing Through Drumming

Bring a drum and beater or rattle to the meeting. Come in silence, and begin beating in steady, even beats, about three beats per second. It's important that the rhythm be relaxed, natural, and easy to play—not too fast and not too slow. The underlying power of this approach is to play in unison, everyone hitting the drumhead or sounding the rattle at the same time.

Some people may have a tendency to go off into their own internal rhythm, thus speeding up the pulse. Resist this tendency if possible, and remember that the focus is to bring everything together.

You must be able to hear your own instrument equally as well as all the others. As the rhythm becomes dependably steady, the body relaxes "into the groove" where your mind focuses on the sound and your spirit is carried effortlessly on the pulsation. If you fall out of the groove, gently bring yourself back to the rhythm. If you can't hear the beat any longer, let your eyes help you synchronize by watching the beat of others.

Drumming in unison provides a rare experience of being very close to others without words. After ten or twenty minutes, without slowing down, let the beat become lighter until it fades away. Remain in the silence for a moment—half a minute or so. Feel the silent pulse continuing to connect you with the others. Feel your heartbeat and the heartbeats of all your friends in the circle. Know that you learned this rhythm from your mother while you nested inside her womb. Know that she learned this rhythm from *her* mother, who learned it from *her* mother . . . who learned it from the Great Mother who gave birth to all.

Developing Trust and Consistency

We've found that having the same people in the circle over a period of time helps to develop trust and consistency. There's an energetic flow among people who sit together over a long period of time. The relationship can then deepen because you will be sharing your joys and pains as they unfold over the years.

Our culture places a high premium on looking good to one another. Rarely do we have a safe place to be witnessed and supported by others, where we can be vulnerable and lay aside our well-practiced facade.

This process is not to be confused with therapy. Stay away from advising other people unless they specifically ask for it. It works best to speak only from our own experience. None of us knows another's path. Providing support by simply witnessing is powerful. However, if it seems that you are moved to do something more, you may ask, "Can I be of help in any way?" This question is respectful of another's process while offering help in a noninvasive way.

When speaking in circle, tell your story as truthfully as you can, and give others your *full* attention. If you do this with the fullness of your being, you most certainly will experience the blessings the circle has to give.

Listening is linked to relationship. It can be done only in the present moment. It gives us energy and regenerates us. True listening lightens our heaviness. So in circle we have the opportunity to know together, to mutually inquire and find our we-ness while not losing our individuality. It is a slow building of shared meaning.

You may feel awkward when you first begin a fellowship. Don't let that get in the way. Just keep meeting, and the benefits will grow and the friendships will become stronger because of your commitment and intention. Follow the energy of the group as it begins to reveal its own integrity.

Emma Guides the Circle

A small group of women—six of us—once met in a clearing in the woods on some private land. Our ages ranged from one and a half to forty-five years. None of us was experienced with intentional circles, but we all brought the commitment of wanting to live in greater balance with ourselves, our families, and the planet that is our shared Mother.

As we stood around a firepit in the late afternoon, I was wondering how we should begin. Someone put on a music tape of women from Ghana singing their traditional songs. It was Emma, the youngest of our group, who first felt the call. Standing there in her diapers, she started drumming the earth with her feet, beating a rhythm to accompany the sounds of the women on the tape. She then bent down and picked up a rattle and added its primeval sound.

As if struck by a thunderbolt, we all got the idea at the same time. With Emma as our guide, we began to peel off and cast aside various layers of clothing until we too were in our "diapers," feeling the warm breezes softly caressing our bareness. We were soon dancing with abandon and playing a jubilee of rattles and drums. Sweet rhythms were coming from deep within each of us as we stomped out a message to the grandmothers: "I am here—I awaken you—I will listen to you."

And a crow gathered the tidbits of mountain gossip as she flew overhead.

For Justine, this gathering took her out of her everyday routine and into nature. But more than that, it was the first time *she* had called for such a gathering. Up until then she had always been dependent on someone else's call to a gathering.

This time she had the need to establish connections from her own wide circle of acquaintances. Some of these women had not known each other before, but the combination was quite dynamic, and even twelve years later they continue to meet on occasion in the circle format. The support of the circle continues to feed Justine's life and work. She has found it to be an endless source of energy that renews and reinspirits her resolve, especially at times of great challenge.

When we recognize the need for fellowship in our own life, then we can draw on the strength of the connections, because we know we're not alone. It is not important to accomplish something explicit, or to even do something useful, because different people will think different things are useful. But synergy will come from cooperating with other elements in the web. Hidden resources become visible and available. We gain strength from our associations and come upon new insights.

The late physicist David Bohm describes the dialogue process: "Some time ago there was an anthropologist who lived a long while with a North American tribe. It was a small group of [forty people]. Now, from time to time that tribe met in a circle. They just talked and talked and talked, apparently to no purpose. They made no decisions. There was no leader. And everybody could participate. There may have been wise men or wise women who were listened to a bit more—the older ones—but everybody could talk. The meeting went on, until it finally seemed to stop for no reason at all and the group dispersed. Yet after that, everybody seemed to know what to do, because they understood one another so well. Then they could get together in smaller groups and do something or decide things."

The circle is a place where people can, in Bohm's words, "think together." It is not about defending an opinion or convincing others; rather, it is a time outside of time to build culture, to strengthen oneself as an individual, and to assist us in being a better part of the collective. All your life and work will be informed and enhanced by this activity.

TEN

Work

as

Service

I slept and dreamt that
   life was joy.
I awoke and saw that life
   was service.
I acted and behold,
   service was joy.
    —RABINDRANATH TAGORE

It is high time the ideal of
success should be replaced
with the ideal of service.
    —ALBERT EINSTEIN

There is a call to us, a call
of service—that we join
with others to try and make
things better in this world.
    —DOROTHY DAY

I don't know what your
destiny will be, but one
thing I do know: the only
ones among you who will
be really happy are those
who have sought and found
how to serve.
    —ALBERT SCHWEITZER

You cannot sincerely help
another without helping
yourself.
    —RALPH WALDO EMERSON

In the Indian classic *Bhagavad Gita*, Krishna says to Arjuna, "Look at me, Arjuna! If I stop working for one moment the whole universe will die. I have nothing to gain from work; I am the sole Lord. But why do I work? Because I love the world." This is compassionate action and serves as the basis of the Eastern tradition known as karma yoga, the practice of work without attachment to the results, and service for the sake of the other.

We live in an interdependent world. Wherever we are, whatever we do, we must keep this global perspective in the forefront of our minds. Joanna Macy, author of *World as Lover, World as Self*, writes, "Everything is interdependent and mutually conditioning—each thought, word, and act, and all beings, too, in the web of life." Just as health care advocates expound on the mind-body link and how our physical condition affects our thinking, so each of us influences the world, and the world in turn has an impact on our personal life.

So, too, are nations interdependent. A rebellion of peasants in Mexico affects the stock market in New York. A contract to build airplanes in China causes workers to lose jobs in the United States. No nation can operate in a vacuum within such a world. Neither can we function without a recognition that our personal behavior is inseparable from our behavior as participants in society. The bad news is that each of us contributes in some measure to the problems in the first place. The good news is that once we realize our link to the problems of the world, we become empowered to contribute toward alleviating them. As we change behavior and perception patterns, so too will the world change.

Work That Makes a Contribution

As we move toward a global society, becoming ever more aware of the sufferings and struggles of the peoples of the Earth, there is more and more reason to recognize the social responsibility each of us has and respond to it. Life is too brief not to. As you're able to do this in daily life, then others may be influenced and inspired to do the same. It's the way the world changes, and each of us makes it happen through what we do.

It is natural to want to serve other people in some meaningful way. The Reverend Mary Manin Morrissey gives an example of this: "I had an experience a number of years ago when I was in the Soviet Union. This was just about a year before the dissolution of the country. We were invited to a Soviet family's home for dinner. They had so little in terms of things as Americans would consider abundance. We climbed sixteen floors to get to their home because the elevator had been out of service for a long time. We had potatoes for dinner, and we had some canned food also. But basically the potatoes were the main dish. Then at dessert time the woman said, 'I have dessert tonight,' and her eyes just lit up. She had stood in line literally for several hours to acquire the dessert for us that night. She then brought out a plate with fresh pears on it. It was like gold. There weren't enough to go around, she didn't eat a pear. I tried to share my pear with her but she wanted *me* to eat this pear. The look on her face and the faces of her family reflected the spirit of generosity, of giving what they had. These people were not poor, these people were wealthy."

We want to help, and are pleased when someone genuinely seeks our support. On the other hand, when we observe the vast human suffering in the world, we may be moved to want to help in some way, but we hold back because of the immensity of the task or because it's easier to remain aloof and not become actively involved. This is the little self or ego-mind seeking self-protection, and it is the root of selfishness. The fact is that when you give of yourself, you receive far more in return.

All of the world's spiritual traditions have stressed the value of compassionate service to alleviate suffering and grow spiritually. Not only does service relieve the suffering of others, it also transforms self-centeredness. In today's world, socially responsible activism and spirituality are becoming more aligned as engaged forms of spiritual practice become more prevalent.

When social and political activism are rooted in spiritual practice, you have the energy and vision to persevere and do whatever is necessary. Though your service may manifest in the external world, this is not an outward path. It is a path guided from within, so that your work becomes like a meditative practice, and your contribution for the benefit of others burns away egocentric motivations. The more you wake up, the more effective your work becomes.

The paradox is that the more active you are in the world, giving freely of yourself, the more deeply you can go into yourself. Gradually, through this process of engagement, you become less attached to whether the results of your actions are successful. As you stay in the present moment and perform your work without imagining a goal in the future, you become more relaxed and less anxious. Success and failure no longer have a hold on you. You are at one with your work and can offer it without any thought of return.

Compassion and Kindness

We all want to contribute, to make a positive difference with our lives. Research and polls have revealed that people who live into their eighties, nineties, and even past a hundred stay healthy and vital because they are doing something meaningful and feel they are making a contribution to others. It is this generosity of spirit we need to carry into our actual work. When our work is motivated by the deep calling to make a contribution, then it is life-affirming and imbued with love. Such work is powerful and compelling. In the giving is the receiving. It's a circle—the energy returns and enables us to continue doing the work.

For us, there is nothing so powerful as having someone tell us how much the radio programming we produce has positively affected and altered his or her life. It reminds us of why we are doing what we do, and inspires us to keep doing it. There is a renewal of commitment.

R. Buckminster Fuller, in his autobiographical book *Critical Path*, writes, "The larger the number for whom I worked, the more positively effective I became. Thus it became obvious that if I worked always and only for all humanity, I would be optimally effective."

Most of us are conditioned to believe that the helper is bestowing some beneficent act on the helped. The fact is that spiritual teachers have always spoken of the true benefit of giving; the real beneficiary is the giver. Swami Vivekananda suggests that we express gratitude for the opportunity to help: "We must remember that it is a privilege to help others. . . . It is not the receiver who is blessed, but it is the giver. Be thankful that you are allowed to exercise your power of benevolence and mercy in the world."

Over the years we have encountered many people who are living their passion through doing work as service. One of those is Bo Lozoff, director of the Human Kindness Foundation and founder of the Prison Ashram Project. He recognized the spiritual need of prisoners and envisioned the idea of helping them to use their cells as ashrams and do their time as "prison monks."

Bo Lozoff's Story

Since 1973 the Prison Ashram Project has sent out hundreds of thousands of books and tapes to prisoners throughout the United States. Bo himself has traveled extensively, giving workshops and classes, visiting prisoners, and working to spawn other projects, study groups, and various resources not only for prisoners but also for their families, prison staff, handicapped people, veterans, and just plain folks.

Bo is not doing this to become famous, make money, or satisfy some self-serving motivation. His inspiration and commitment come from genuine, heartfelt compassion, and he's willing to do whatever it takes to get the job done.

This is not an easy path, particularly at a time when the United States now imprisons more of its citizens per capita than any other nation on Earth. There is an outcry for harsher treatment of prisoners, and more money is being expended for prisons than for education. Yet Bo can say, "Working with prisoners is joyous work. Being involved in their lives, after they've possibly done horrible things and had horrible things done to them, at a time in which they decide to seek something deeper, higher, is the greatest honor, the greatest privilege, as that transformation occurs."

Bucky Fuller's Story

We were privileged to spend time over several years with the late R. Buckminster Fuller. He was someone who overcame all odds to do what he accomplished, and was called "the planet's friendly genius."

In 1927, when he was thirty-two years old, he reached a turning point. His young daughter had just died, the building company he headed was bankrupt, he was in disgrace and utterly broke. He found himself contemplating suicide on the shore of Lake Michigan in Chicago, where he and his family lived.

Bucky recalls, "I stood by the side of the lake, hesitating. All my life, at home and in school, I had been admonished: 'Never mind what you think! Listen! We are trying to teach you!' I asked myself what a little, penniless human being with a remaining life expectancy of only ten years — the life expectancy then of those born, as I was, in 1895 was forty-two — could do for humanity that great corporations and great political states cannot do. Answering myself, I said: 'The individual can take initiative without anyone's permission.'

"I told myself: 'You do not have the right to eliminate yourself; you do not belong to you. You belong to the universe. This significance of you will remain obscure to you, but you may assume that you are fulfilling your significance if you apply yourself to converting all your experience to the highest advantage of others!'

"So I vowed to keep myself alive, but only if I would never use me again for just me—each one of us is born of two, and we really belong to each other. I vowed to do my own thinking, instead of trying to accommodate everyone else's opinions, credos and theories. I vowed to apply my inventory of experiences to the solving of problems that affect everyone aboard planet Earth."

Bucky lived another fifty-six years, and was eighty-seven when he died in 1983. He traveled millions of miles with his powerful message that there is a scientific, natural order and purpose underlying the vision of one world, one vast pool of resources, one economy, and one potentially successful human race.

According to Bucky, the world can work for everyone. We have to redirect our priorities. His work was driven by the vision of a larger reality, a greater intelligence operating in the universe. By the shores of Lake Michigan he set a lifelong commitment for himself based on serving something bigger than he was and at the same time serving his fellow humans. Reflecting on his life, Bucky said, "Many times I've chickened, and everything inevitably goes wrong. But then, when I return to my commitment, my life suddenly works again. There's something of the miraculous in that."

Rosita Arvigo's Story

A few years ago we met Dr. Rosita Arvigo, who was born in the United States and trained as a doctor of naprapathy, and is an herbologist now living in Belize. For ten years she studied with Don Elijio Panti, now more than a hundred years old and one of the last surviving and most respected traditional healers in Central America. She describes this experience in her book *Sastun: My Apprenticeship with a Maya Healer.*

Rosita is a dynamo with the energy of ten activists. Her original intent was to learn more about the native plants of Belize. What she discovered instead was her life's work — the quest to sustain and study rain forest plants and bridge the gap between Panti's native wisdom and modern healing practices.

She founded the Ix Chel Tropical Research Foundation, which has sent over two thousand plants to the National Cancer Institute; twelve of these plants have proven particularly promising and are under serious study for the treatment of cancer and other diseases for which modern medicine has yet to find a cure. She also created the Panti Maya Medicine Trail, which identifies thirty-five of the most useful plants growing wild in the rain forest. Schoolchildren, tourists, scientists, and health professionals regularly visit the trail, the first of its kind in Central America.

Arvigo has set up conferences throughout Belize where healers can meet and exchange their knowledge and experience. This has resulted in the formation of the Belize Association of Traditional Healers. For the first time, this fragmented group of healers can share their invaluable knowledge with their peers.

Dr. Arvigo is the director of the six-thousand-acre Terra Nova Medicinal Plant Reserve, which guarantees that future generations of healers will have medicinal plants to harvest and serves as a home for seedlings rescued from destruction. In addition, Dr. Arvigo cofounded Rainforest Remedies, a profit-sharing company that makes herbal tinctures from rain forest plants about to be destroyed. She has involved at-risk urban youth in recovering medicinal plants from condemned land in a creative cooperation that focuses their youthful energy into a productive and positive direction.

Rosita Arvigo is someone who is living her passion through a life of work as service. Her approach to work is rooted in many of the principles already presented in this book. She says, "When you're in synch, in harmony with nature and a positive flow, trying to create solutions rather than getting lost in the problems, things seem to move of their own accord. You get in that positive stance and you stay there, and step by step you seem to really bring about a change and develop something."

Joe Dominguez's Story

In 1984 Michael attended a seminar at the suggestion of a longtime listener of New Dimensions. It was entitled "Transforming Your Relationship with Money and Achieving Financial Independence," and the presenter was Joe Dominguez. Small, wiry, and dynamic, Joe proceeded to carefully map out a logical and reasonable method for attaining the lofty goal implied by the title of his workshop. Prior to attending, Michael assumed that one of the ways Joe achieved financial independence was by getting thousands of people to fork out money to attend the seminar. Much to Michael's happy surprise, he learned that Joe took no revenue from the seminars, but instead gave it away to worthy causes through a nonprofit organization called the New Road Map Foundation. He lived very frugally on about six thousand dollars per year, which was the interest he received from bonds he had purchased many years before, when he quit being a Wall Street stockbroker. After several years of presenting the seminar he created a set of tapes based on it and proceeded to sell thousands of them, helping many people to transform their relationship with money. The seminars and tapes eventually led to a best-selling book, *Your Money or Your Life*, written by Joe and his partner, Vicki Robin.

The key point here is that Joe Dominguez created his life in such a way as to jump off the consumerist merry-go-round, live simply but richly, and give of his expertise to others in a manner that enabled him to donate large sums of money to people and organizations making positive contributions to the world. As he said, "I had concluded that life was not about making money; so what was it about? After a year and a half and a lot of introspection, I came to the conclusion that what my personal life was about was to serve, to serve the planet."

Darca Nicholson's Story

When we left urban San Francisco and moved to rural Mendocino County, a little more than a hundred miles north, to live in a cooperative land project with three other couples, it was a major leap. In a relatively small community where neighbors may share stream water, access roads, garden produce, plumbing tips, and tools and techniques for more humane living, the word gets around about those individuals who are committed helpers and servers. These dedicated persons give freely of their time and energy to be of service however they can. One of those we first heard about was Darca Nicholson. At the time she was involved in cocreating a cooperative community on a sizeable piece of land and had been suggested to us as someone with expertise and experience in creating new and experimental community-living enterprises. Additionally, she was a professional masseuse whose reputation and skill as a bodyworker preceded her. We eventually came to know Darca and learned that she was a native of Iowa who had helped found the first women's health clinic in that state. Now, in the midst of a busy professional schedule and raising a daughter, she works tirelessly and without any fanfare to enable people to network with one another, and often serves behind the scenes as a mediator in disputes and as a volunteer for numerous important and socially relevant community projects and causes. She gives of herself without thought of reward or acknowledgment, and therein lies her power to make a difference. Darca Nicholson represents thousands of unsung community heroes and heroines who do so much to enhance and amplify community life the world over.

The Moral

Each of these individuals recognized that he or she was part of a larger human community and a greater force operating in the universe. When you feel yourself part of this extraordinary human family, then you can connect with compassion to your fellow humans and discover the ways you can be of service. Look around you and see what needs doing—and then commit yourself to satisfying that need. Such an act will open the doors to your own life purpose, and you will begin to realize your full potential.

According to the ancient Indian sage Patanjali, "When you are inspired by some great purpose, some extraordinary project, all your thoughts break their bounds: Your mind transcends limitations, your consciousness expands in every direction, and you find yourself in a new, great, and wonderful world. Dormant forces, faculties, and talents come alive, and you discover yourself to be a greater person by far than you ever dreamed yourself to be."

There is so much to be done; the opportunities are limitless. What do you want to give to the world? What moves you? Where do you feel inspired to serve? Listen to your inner voice and pay attention to the world around you. You have very special gifts to offer. Use your imagination and your intellect to discover what they are.

You will discover your passion by uncovering your compassion, your own sense of connection to others. The word *compassion* means "with passion." Compassion is a deeply felt resonance with humanity and the natural world. With it comes purpose, and the two combine to create work as service.

Whatever work you are doing or may choose to do in the future, remember always that you are connected to the whole world and even the smallest act makes a difference. Gandhi said, "What you do may seem insignificant, but it's very important that you do it." Just as mathematicians have shown that the flapping of a butterfly's wing in Japan can affect the weather in New York City, so too does your work affect the rest of the planet. How you do your work matters to all of us, and especially to yourself. You alone are the creator of true work.

Epilogue
True Work Circles

Manifesting true work may not be convenient, nor will it always be easy. As we strive to make our work more unified with our life, and introduce more fun and meaning into both, we need support. It is through connecting with others that we will receive this support to move into a new model of work and play. We highly recommend that you get together with other people who want to express their passion, increase their joy, act with authenticity, pursue their deepest longings, and create meaning through their work. We suggest that you form a *True Work Circle* to strengthen your efforts to inspirit your work.

Invite friends and acquaintances to join with you in meeting regularly. A group of five to seven people holding one another's dreams and visions in their hearts will produce miracles of manifestation. The *True Work Circle* is a place to give voice to your deepest longings and worst fears. When your hopes and intentions are shared with others in a sacred and respectful way everyone is empowered and you will discover new opportunities of expression.

The context of work and business is changing for the better. There are many signs that indicate spirit is emerging in the workplace. As we practice honesty, respect, openness, compassion, commitment to quality, concern for the environment, and connectedness with one another, so will the workplace become a place of growing spirit as well. We all recognize when these qualities are absent, so we must encourage one another to develop a spiritual consciousness in our everyday work. As we sit together in mutual support and practice nonjudgmental listening and sharing, we can relearn how to be creative instead of reactive.

When we began presenting seminars on work we found that people were inspired by talking about their dreams and visions of what work can be. Gathering together in small coteries will support the creative inquiry of working with passion. The benefits of reflecting with others are enormous. It will keep you "on the road" of following your true work.

A *True Work Circle* strives for deep dialogue. The difference between dialogue and ordinary discussion is that in discussion people usually hold a firm position and argue in favor of their pre-conceived views as they try to convince others to see it their way. Dialogue, on the other hand, precludes trying to win someone over to one's viewpoint. There is a shared spirit of support and cooperation.

Guidelines for Forming a True Work Circle

If you would like to form a *True Work Circle,* here are some suggestions on how to begin. These steps will help to get you started, but the circle will be uniquely formed by the people who choose to participate.

We recommend the size be moderate (five to seven people) so that everyone has time to speak. Invite people who care about following their passion and developing more meaningful work. It's best to find your circle mates by direct contact rather than putting out a public notice. Trust builds over time. It is good to have the same people week after week.

If you must add new people, do it slowly, one at a time. It takes time for a new participant to become integrated and feel at ease within a group that is already established and has built some history together.

Meeting once a week for two to four hours is optimal, but meeting twice a month can also be beneficial. Everyone must commit to making a priority to arrive on time, and stay to the end. We suggest that you make a commitment to meet for nine months. This is the natural human gestation period and will provide sufficient time to experience a difference in your life and work. Some groups meet once a month, but they meet for an entire day, so that the number of hours turns out to be the same as if they were meeting every week. It's best to keep it simple and not require people to bring food or snacks. You'll find that it will be easier for people to keep their commitment if the circle gets right to its purpose and ends on time, so that they can return home at a reasonable hour, especially if you hold the circle on a week night. If you allow the circle to drift, without a specific time for closure, then some people will choose not to continue. The *True Work Circle* is based upon the principle of communion, which is mutual agreement based on consent. It is important that everyone can support all the decisions of the group.

Create a safe group container. Select an appropriate place, one that provides privacy and is free from outside distractions and interruptions. It can be in someone's home or it can be a small room provided by a church or civic group. It's important to sit in a circle, whether on chairs or on the floor with pillows. Sit so that everyone can see everyone else's face, because this fosters a commonality and equality.

Establish a sense of ritual and acknowledgment of the spiritual. This can take the form of anything that the group agrees on, but it is wise to keep it simple. Here are some suggestions:

- Light a candle and have a moment of silent prayer or invite one person to say a prayer for the group, giving thanks and asking for spirit to be present. It's better for a different person to offer the prayer each week. Another way to call in spirit is to let the prayer move aloud around the circle, each person adding their expression.

- Arrange a group of candles (one for each person in the group) around a vase of flowers. Have everyone light a candle and ask for some quality to be present, such as clarity, courage, innocence, change, beauty, compassion, wisdom, joy, and inspiration.

- Hold hands and chant together, and follow with five minutes of meditation.

- Each week ask a different person to bring an inspiring reading or a poem to share at the beginning.

Any of these will help to mark this time as special and important. Whatever you choose to do, keep in mind that it will set the tone for this precious time you spend together. It will also help to separate it from the rest of your day. Acknowledging your connection with the Divine, the Great Mystery, God, Goddess, (or whatever term works for you) opens the meeting to our connection with the spiritual dimension of life.

Close the meeting with a short ritual. Each participant might give a brief prayer of thanks for the time spent together and for the support from the group, as well as the invisible forces that surround it with loving presence. If you have lit candles, take this time to blow them out one by one as each person expresses gratitude.

Advice for Building a Strong True Work Circle

Success is dependent on the amount of energy, attention, and compassion that each is willing to give to the process of the circle. It is a gathering based on goodheartedness. When speaking, speak to everyone in the circle and listen with alert attention to each person as they share. An invisible field of energy is created by everyone being mindful and attentive to everyone else. You never know from where your own insights will come. Care-full, compassionate listening provides an atmosphere for new things to be said. When people are truly listening, you will often find yourself saying things you've never said before.

Come to the circle with an "I don't know attitude." It takes a willingness to let go of a particular mindset and belief system to be open to new ideas. Some would say, "Empty your cup so it may be filled." Stay in the present. Listen with an open mind, without judging. Don't rush to respond, but allow yourself to go slowly, so that the deeper truths can emerge. It is a place to inquire, explore, and investigate your longings, hopes, and dreams in the company of others.

Be open to surprise and incorporate a sense of play and good cheer. This is meant to be a creative, enjoyable, and ful-filling activity.

Become aware of the special gifts of each person in the

group and support each member in the expression of those gifts. Learn to be together in the full radiance of the beauty of who you are. As one person in the group makes a breakthrough in his or her work, it encourages everyone to keep to the path of expressing their own dreams and visions. Each person brings a strand of wisdom, and together you will form a new tapestry.

You must be vigilant to keep the dialogue from becoming a therapy session. Be careful not to allow one person to monopolize or dominate the conversation. Keep to the agreed-upon topic and do not get off on another agenda. A diversity of opinions is both healthy and stimulating. See differing viewpoints as an opportunity for learning and deepening the dialogue. The process is meant to be collaborative and not confrontational. When you invest in the process through active listening—really hearing what others say—the dialogue will be more engaging and you will learn more.

Someone may have a specific perspective, but it is important not to be locked into it. People can disagree without someone having to be wrong. The purpose is to share. Always speak from direct experience rather than giving advice. In circle, you are holding what everyone is saying without having to arrive at an overall conclusion. Let the paradoxical linger until it naturally progresses into a larger view. Allow yourself to be comfortable with loose ends. Rest in the territory of whatever it is you are exploring until you fully know it.

The wisdom of the circle will come forth as you create a history of mutual respect, nonjudgmental listening, and honest sharing.

Some Suggested Activities and Questions

Here are a few questions and activities to help the group start exploring true work. Each of these questions can be a whole session or two.

- Take some quiet time to go back in your memory to when you were very young, and think of one or two activities that you loved. These would be moments when time sped by without your being conscious of it, when you were so absorbed in the doing that all else disappeared. Share the memory with the group. Express the feeling of it. Help them to know the joy you experienced.

- Describe the history of your work experience. Go back to your earliest jobs. They could be jobs you did as a child around the house, then later, jobs you did for money. What were some of your earliest money-earning endeavors? Did you sell Girl Scout cookies or magazines for your school? How did you feel about it? Recall your various work environments and the attitude you had toward them.

- Talk about what you would love to be doing more of in your life. Can you do it in your present work situation?

- By what criteria do you measure success and wealth?

- What is the overall environment of your present workplace?

- How do you imagine your ideal work environment? Be expansive and generous with yourself. Allow your deepest longings to come forth.

- What are your concerns about work?

- What experiences have influenced your opinion about work?

- Are you finding meaning in your work? If not, why not?

- Some of the changes you may want to see at work are: a lessening of the us/them dynamic; more fun; more use of your creative instincts; an emotionally safe work environment for everybody; being fully alive in your work; making it a place where the emotional, psychological, and spiritual dimension is respected.

- Engage in group brainstorming about how to transform your vision into reality. Listen and respond to one another. Learn from others what has worked for them and what has not. Share your obstacles, opportunities, and dreams as clearly as possible.

- Each week tell the group what you intend to do in the coming week to further your expression of your true work. It is best to use the wisdom of baby steps. Keep the activity manageable. If you try to take too big a leap and it doesn't work out, discouragement may result. Keep in mind that doing something regularly to attain your vision, no matter how small, will build up to something big in less time than you imagine. Having a check-in with the group about the past week's activity helps them hold your vision in their hearts. Knowing you will be checking in with the group will help you maintain your focus through the week. Use the wisdom of the group to help you.

Change is a process that happens over time. Be patient with yourself and others. True work comes with time and perseverance.

If you are interested in forming a *True Work Circle* and want additional information, write to: *True Work Circles*, New Dimensions Radio, P.O. Box 569, Ukiah, CA 95482 or call (707) 468-5215.

E-mail: ndradio@igc.org

Website: http://www.newdimensions.org

Bibliography

Bloom, William. *Money, Heart and Mind: Financial Well-Being for People and Planet.* Kodansha America, Inc., 1996.

Bohm, David. *On Dialogue.* [Pamphlet] David Bohm Seminars, 1990. (Available through P.O. Box 1452, Ojai, CA 93023.)

Bohm, David, and F. David Peat. *Science, Order and Creativity.* Bantam, 1987.

Boldt, Laurence G. *Zen and the Art of Making a Living.* Arkana, 1993.

Cahill, Sedonia, Charles Garfield, and Cindy Spring. *Wisdom Circles: A Guide to Self-Discovery and Building Community in Small Groups.* Hyperion, 1998.

Cahill, Sedonia, and Joshua Halpern. *Ceremonial Circle: Practice, Ritual, and Renewal for Personal and Community Healing.* HarperSanFrancisco, 1992.

Cameron, Julia. *The Artist's Way: A Spiritual Path to Higher Creativity.* Jeremy P. Tarcher, Inc., 1992.

———. *Vein of Gold: A Journey to Your Creative Heart.* Jeremy P. Tarcher/Putnam, 1996.

Campbell, Joseph. *The Hero with a Thousand Faces.* Princeton University Press, 1972.

———. *An Open Life: Joseph Campbell in Conversation with Michael Toms.* Edited by Dennie Briggs and John Maher. HarperCollins, 1990.

———. *A Joseph Campbell Companion: Reflections on the Art of Living.* Edited by Diane K. Osbon. HarperCollins, 1991.

Chaudhuri, Haridas. *Integral Yoga.* Routledge, 1990.

Chopra, Deepak. *The Path to Love: Renewing the Power of Spirit in Your Life.* Harmony Books, 1997.

Covey, Stephen, Roger A. Merrill, and Rebecca R. Merrill. *First Things First.* Simon and Schuster, 1994.

Diaz, Adriana. *Freeing the Creative Spirit.* HarperSanFrancisco, 1992.

Dominguez, Joe, and Vicki Robin. *Your Money or Your Life: Transforming Your Relationship with Money and Achieving Financial Independence.* Viking Penguin, 1992.

Dyer, Wayne. *Real Magic: Creating Miracles in Everyday Life.* HarperCollins, 1992.

Fields, Rick, Peggy Taylor, Rex Weyler, and Rick Ingrasci. *Chop Wood, Carry Water: A Guide to Finding Spiritual Fulfillment in Everyday Life.* Jeremy P. Tarcher, Inc., 1984.

Fox, Matthew. *The Reinvention of Work: A New Vision of Livelihood for Our Time.* HarperSanFrancisco, 1994.

Fuller, R. Buckminster. *A Critical Path.* St. Martin's Press, 1981.

Hakim, Cliff. *We Are All Self-Employed.* Berrett-Kohler Publishers, Inc., 1994.

Houston, Jean. *The Possible Human.* Jeremy P. Tarcher, Inc., 1982.

Hwoschinsky, Paul. *True Wealth.* Ten Speed Press, 1990.

I Ching, or Book of Changes. Translated by C. F. Baynes and Richard Wilhelm. Princeton University Press, 1967.

Kabat-Zinn, Jon. *Wherever You Go, There You Are.* Hyperion, 1995.

Krishnamurti, J. *Think on These Things.* Edited by D. Rajagopal. Harper and Row, 1970.

———. *The First and Last Freedom.* Harper and Row, 1975.

Leider, Richard J., and David A. Shapiro. *Repacking Your Bags: Lighten Your Load for the Rest of Your Life.* Berrett-Kohler Publishers, Inc., 1995.

Mindell, Arnold. *Leader as Martial Artist: An Introduction to Deep Democracy.* HarperSanFrancisco, 1992

Moore, Thomas. *Care of the Soul: A Guide for Cultivating Depth and Sacredness in Everyday Life.* HarperCollins, 1992.

———. *The Re-Enchantment of Everyday Life.* HarperCollins, 1996.

Morrissey, Mary Manin. *Building Your Field of Dreams.* Bantam, 1996.

Moss, Richard. *The Second Miracle: Intimacy, Spirituality, and Conscious Relationship.* Celestial Arts, 1995.

Needleman, Jacob. *Money and the Meaning of Life.* Doubleday, 1991.

Orsborn, Carol. *Inner Excellence: Spiritual Principles of Life-Driven Business.* New World Library, 1992.

Patent, Arnold. *Money and Beyond.* Celebration Publishing, 1993.

Phillips, Michael. *The Seven Laws of Money.* Word Wheel/Random House, 1974.

Prabhavananda, Swami. *The Sermon on the Mount According to Vedanta.* New American Library, 1963.

Prabhavananda, Swami, and Christopher Isherwood. *The Song of God: Bhagavad Gita.* Vedanta Press, 1967.

Ram Dass, and Mirabai Bush. *Compassion in Action: Setting Out on the Path of Service.* Bell Tower, 1992.

Ray, Michael, and Lorna Catford. *The Path of the Everyday Hero.* Jeremy P. Tarcher, Inc., 1991.

Sher, Barbara. *I Could Do Anything If I Only Knew What It Was.* Delacorte Press, 1994.

————. *Live the Life You Love.* Delacorte Press, 1996.

Siegel, Bernie. *How to Live Between Office Visits: A Guide to Life, Love and Health.* HarperCollins, 1993.

Sinetar, Marsha. *Do What You Love, the Money Will Follow.* Dell, 1987.

————. *To Build the Life You Want, Create the Work You Want.* St. Martin's Press, 1995.

Singer, June. *Seeing Through the Visible World: Jung, Gnosis and Chaos.* Harper and Row, 1990.

Sogyal Rinpoche. *The Tibetan Book of Living and Dying.* Harper-SanFrancisco, 1992.

Tart, Charles T. *Living the Mindful Life.* Shambhala Publications, 1994.

Tarthang Tulku. *Mastering Successful Work.* Dharma Publishing, 1994.

Thich Nhat Hanh. *Being Peace.* Parallax Press, 1987.

van der Post, Laurens. *Feather Fall.* William Morrow and Co., Inc., 1994.

Vivekananda, Swami. *Karma Yoga and Bhakti Yoga.* Ramakrishna-Vivekananda Center, 1955.

Whyte, David. *The Heart Aroused: Poetry and the Preservation of the Soul in Corporate America.* Doubleday, 1994.

Wing, R. L. *The I Ching Workbook.* Doubleday and Co., 1979.

Index

Index

purpose,
    and deepest longings, 45
    clarity of, 26

Radha, Swami Sivananda, 117, 133
radical trust, 45, 60, 61
Ramakrishna, Sri, 144, 145
Rechtschaffen, Stephan, 137
retreats, 83
risk taking, 45, 60
Robin, Vicki, 155, 186
Robinson, Jonathan, 30
"rules" breaking down, 21, 22

sanuk, 26
Schopenhauer, Arthur, 25
Schwarz, Jack, 53
Schweitzer, Albert, 176
security as illusion, 22
Shabistarî, 162
Shakespeare, 88
Sher, Barbara, 97, 98
Siegel, Bernie, 92
Sills, Beverly, 90
Sinetar, Marsha, 17, 149
Singer, June, 94, 170
single focus, 115, 116
Sivaraksa, Sulak, 26
Sogyal Rinpoche, 101, 118, 119, 133
solitude, 84
soul,
    and money, 152, 153
    embracing it wholly, 23
    fulfilling purpose of, 41
    meaningful contribution, 27
    moments, 24, 25
    purpose and intention, 115
    relative vs. absolute level, 101
    resides, 101
spaciousness of mind, 101
Spiegelberg, Frederick, 141, 142
spirit, 17
spontaneity, 77
Spretnak, Charlene, 118
Starhawk, 162

Steindl-Rast, David, 148
Sun, Patricia, 73, 128
Suzuki, Shunryu, 73
synchronicity, 54, 55, 57

Tagore, Rabindranath, 176
Tara, 142–144
Tarthang Tulku, 73
Tart, Charles, 29
teleology, 113
Terkel, Studs, 49
Thich Nhat Hanh, 66
Thomas, Gyen, 133
true work, 26, 27, 40, 189
Twist, Lynne, 152, 153

Ueland, Brenda, 49, 88
unification experience, 80

van der Post, Sir Laurens, 16, 159,
    163
Vivekananda, Swami, 13, 61, 144,
    181

Wagner, Jane, 90
Walker, Alice, 43
Walsch, Neale Donald, 105
Weil, Simone, 127
welcoming the unexpected, 44–48
wisdom vs. information, 140, 141
work,
    and the invisible world, 130
    as art or craft, 130
    as passion, 39, 40
    as play, 70–72
    as spiritual practice, 128
    as toxic, 102
    as unifying, 26, 27
    essential principles of, 31, 32
    new world of, 21, 45
    spiritual principles within, 104
    Tao of, 78, 79
worker dissatisfaction, 21

Zohar, Danah, 163

About New Dimensions®

Since 1973 Justine and Michael Toms have been presenting leading thinkers, social innovators, scientists, and creative artists through New Dimensions Radio. The programming supports a diversity of views from many traditions and cultures and fosters the purpose of living a healthier life of mind, body, and spirit while deepening connections to self, family, community, environment, and planet.

If you would like to find out more about the work of New Dimensions Radio, please write or call and request a free audiotape catalog, a complimentary issue of the bimonthly *New Dimensions Journal*, and a brochure.

New Dimensions Radio
Dept. TW
P.O. Box 569
Ukiah, CA 95482
Telephone: (707) 468-9830
E-mail: ndradio@igc.org
Website: http://www.newdimensions.org

About the Authors

Michael Toms is the founding president of New Dimensions Foundation, cofounder of New Dimensions Radio, and chief executive officer of the New Dimensions Broadcasting Network. Educated in broadcasting at the University of Miami, he went on to postgraduate work in psychology and the philosophy of religion. He serves as the executive producer and principal host of *New Dimensions,* the award-winning and widely praised syndicated radio series; he has spent more than twenty-five years exploring creative ideas with many of the most interesting people of our time, and is acknowledged as one of the premier interviewers in media today. His book *An Open Life: Joseph Campbell in Conversation with Michael Toms* was nationally acclaimed. He is the recipient of two honorary doctorates for his vanguard work in media and is an adjunct professor at Union Graduate School and Marylhurst Graduate School of Business. A writer, seminar leader, and consultant for communications, marketing, and fundraising, he has worked with literally hundreds of organizations. He also served for seven years as senior acquisitions editor for HarperSanFrancisco and is board chairman emeritus of the California Institute of Integral Studies.

Justine Willis Toms is cofounder and executive director of New Dimensions Radio and serves as managing producer and music director of the *New Dimensions* radio series. For more than twenty-five years she has worked with many of the leading thinkers, spiritual teachers, social architects, scientists, and creative artists of the late twentieth century. Her keen interest in nontraditional education and innovative learning techniques has helped to create the natural ambiance and engaging style of *New Dimensions* broadcast programming and audiotapes. A graduate of Auburn University, she serves as editor in chief of *New Dimensions Journal*, a bimonthly national publication based on the work of New Dimensions Radio. She is director emeritus of the Association for Transpersonal Psychology. Together with her partner, Michael, she lives in a rural setting in Mendocino County, northern California, where they pursue true work, living close to nature and managing a global broadcast organization.